VOWEL SOUNDS

Symbol	Examples	Symbol	Examples
a	act, bat	b	back, cab
ā	day, age	ch	cheap, match, picture
âr	air, dare	d	door, head
ä	father, star	f	fan, leaf, phone
e	edge, ten	g	give, dog
ē	speed, money	h	her, behave
ə*	ago, system, easily, compete, focus	j	just, page
		k	king, bake, car
ēr	dear, pier	l	leaf, roll
i	fit, is	m	my, home
ī	sky, bite	n	note, rain
o	not, wasp	ng	sing, bank
ō	nose, over	p	put, stop
ô	law, order	r	red, far
oi	noise, enjoy	s	say, pass
o͞o	true, boot	sh	ship, push
oo	put, look	t	to, let
yo͞o	cute, united	th	thin, with
ou	loud, cow	TH	THat, baTHe
u	fun, up	v	value, live
ûr	learn, urge, butter, word	w	want, away
		y	yes, onion
		z	zoo, maze, rise
		zh	pleasure, vision

*This symbol, the *schwa*, represents the sound of unaccented vowels. It sounds like "uh."

Why Do You Need this New Edition?

If you're wondering why you should buy this new edition of *Active Vocabulary*, here are 8 good reasons!

1. **Eighteen new vocabulary words** for you to master and apply to your everyday life.

2. **Seven new or updated engaging readings** introduce you to the vocabulary words and allow you to exercise your vocabulary skills.

3. **Two additional Review Chapters** for you to test your mastery of key words.

4. **Two new collaborative activities** in the Review Chapters, entitled "Mix It Up," so that you can work with classmates to develop your vocabulary skills.

5. New **"Conversation Starters"** and **"Word Part Reminders"** to help you remember the vocabulary words you were taught earlier in the chapter.

6. The **Analogy Self-Tests** have been moved to the latter part of each chapter to allow you to work with key words first before encountering this challenging activity.

7. A new **Glossary** has been added for easy reference to the vocabulary words.

8. A new **Web site**, replacing the CD-ROM, has been developed for additional practice.

Active Vocabulary

General and Academic Words

Fourth Edition

Amy E. Olsen
Cuesta College

Longman

New York   San Francisco   Boston
London   Toronto   Sydney   Tokyo   Singapore   Madrid
Mexico City   Munich   Paris   Cape Town   Hong Kong   Montreal

Acquisitions Editor: Kate Edwards
Marketing Manager: Thomas DeMarco
Senior Supplements Editor: Donna Campion
Senior Media Producer: Stefanie Liebman
Production Manager: Savoula Amanatidis
Project Coordination, Text Design, and Electronic Page Makeup: Elm Street Publishing Services
Cover Design Manager: Wendy Ann Fredericks
Cover Designer: Nancy Sacks
Cover Photos: Amy E. Olsen
Photo Researcher: Linda Sykes
Senior Manufacturing Buyer: Dennis J. Para
Printer and Binder: Quebecor World Book Services—Dubuque
Cover Printer: Lehigh-Phoenix Color Corporation

Photo Credits: **p. 1 (T, B):** Amy E. Olsen; **p. 1 (M):** SPL/Photo Researchers, Inc.; **p. 12:** Amy E. Olsen; **p.16:** Chabruken/Getty Images; **p. 22 (T):** Burke/Triolo Productions/Foodpix/Jupiter Images; **p. 22 (B):** Ellen Setisi/The Image Works; **p. 24:** Mike Howell/Stone/Getty Images; **p. 26 (T):** Amy E. Olsen; **p. 26 (B):** Janis Cristie/Getty Images RF; **p. 30:** Amy E. Olsen; **p. 36:** Amy E. Olsen; **p. 40:** SPL/Photo Researchers, Inc.; **p. 44:** Don Klumpp/Getty Images; **p. 46:** Michael Newman/PhotoEdit, Inc.; **p. 54:** Amy E. Olsen; **p. 60:** Amy E. Olsen; **p. 66:** Amy E. Olsen; **p. 69:** Amy E. Olsen; **p. 71 (T):** Bob Daemmrich/The Image Works; **p. 71 (M):** China Span/Getty Images; **p. 71 (B):** Tony Olsen; **p. 72:** Bob Daemmrich/The Image Works; **p. 74:** Amy E. Olsen; **p. 78 (T):** China Span/Getty Images; **p. 78 (B):** Wildlife/Peter Arnold, Inc.; **p. 81:** Corbis; **p. 86:** Amy E. Olsen; **p. 90:** Amy E. Olsen; **p. 92:** Amy E. Olsen; **p. 94:** Vic Bider/PhotoEdit, Inc.; **p. 98:** Amy E. Olsen; **p. 104:** Amy E. Olsen; **p. 108:** Tony Olsen; **p. 110:** Hulton Archive/Getty Images; **p. 112 (L):** Amy E. Olsen; **p. 112 (R):** Tony Olsen; **p. 114:** Jim Zuckerman/Corbis; **p. 116:** Tony Olsen; **p. 120 (T):** Bettmann/Corbis; **p. 120 (B):** Corbis; **p. 122:** Tony Olsen; **p. 123:** Paul Schmeister/Corbis; **p. 126:** Mark Richards/PhotoEdit, Inc.; **p. 128 (T):** Amy E. Olsen; **p. 128 (B):** Stephen Ferry/Redux; **p. 129:** Nicholas Sapieha/The Art Archive; **p. 134 (T):** Amy E. Olsen; **p. 134 (B):** Amy E. Olsen; **p. 137:** Amy E. Olsen; **p. 138 (T):** Karen Preuss/The Image Works; **p. 138 (B):** Dagmar Ehling/Photo Researchers, Inc.; **p. 144 (T):** Tony Olsen; **p. 144 (B):** Amy E. Olsen; **p. 146:** Gerald Warnken, Jr.; **p. 147:** Tony Olsen; **p. 150:** Mauro Fermariello/Photo Researchers, Inc.; **p. 153:** Bettmann/Corbis; **p. 156 (T):** Gjon Mili/Getty Images; **p. 156 (B):** Ronnie Kamen/PhotoEdit, Inc.; **p. 159:** Milt Olsen; **p. 164:** Amy E. Olsen

Copyright © 2010 by Pearson Education, Inc.

1 2 3 4 5 6 7 8 9 10—QWD—12 11 10 09

Longman
is an imprint of

www.pearsonhighered.com

ISBN-10:   0-205-63273-4
ISBN-13: 978-0-205-63273-2

Dedication

To Gerry, Bartleby, Tony, Katy, Danny, Matty, and Keri
Loads of thanks, fellow Eastsiders, for fun times and great memories.

—*Amy E. Olsen*

Contents

PART I GENERAL WORDS

SECTION I Student Life

SECTION II Reading for Pleasure

PART II   ACADEMIC WORDS

Preface

Because students benefit greatly from increased word power, the study of vocabulary should be enjoyable. Unfortunately, vocabulary workbooks often lose sight of this goal. To help make the study of vocabulary an exciting and enjoyable part of college study, I have written *Active Vocabulary*.

The goal of this book—the second in a three-book interactive vocabulary series—is to make the study of vocabulary fun through a variety of thematic readings, self-tests, and interactive exercises. As a casual glimpse through the book will indicate, these activities involve writing, personal experience, art, and many other formats. The goal of these activities is simple: to utilize individual learning styles in order to help students learn new words in a large number of contexts.

Underlying the text's strong visual appeal is a central philosophy: an essential part of learning vocabulary is repeated exposure to a word. *Active Vocabulary* provides eight exposures to each word in the text plus more opportunities for exposure through the Collaborative Activities and games in the *Instructor's Manual*.

Content Overview

Active Vocabulary is an ideal text for both classroom and self-study. The eighteen main chapters follow a specific and consistent format.

- **Thematic Reading:** Because most vocabulary is acquired through reading, each chapter, with the exception of the Word Parts and Review Chapters, begins with a thematic reading that introduces ten vocabulary words in context. These readings come in a variety of formats, from newspaper reviews to journal entries. The goal is to show that new words may be encountered anywhere. Rather than simply presenting a word list with definitions, students have the opportunity to discover the meanings of these new words via context clues.

  The themes for *Active Vocabulary* were chosen from areas most interesting to students of all ages and from disciplines that most students will encounter at some point in their college careers. In choosing the words, I've been guided by five factors: (1) relation to the chapter theme, (2) use in popular magazines, newspapers, novels, and textbooks, (3) occurrence in standardized tests such as the SAT and GRE, (4) containing word parts introduced in the text, and (5) my experiences teaching in developmental reading and writing classrooms.

- **Predicting:** The second page of each chapter contains a Predicting activity that gives students the chance to figure out the meaning of each vocabulary word before looking at its definition. The Predicting section helps students learn the value of context clues in determining a word's meaning. While the text does offer information on dictionary use, I strongly advocate the use of context clues as one of the most active methods of vocabulary development.

- **Self-Tests:** Following the Predicting activity are three Self-Tests in various formats. With these tests, students can monitor their comprehension. The tests include text and sentence completion, true/false situations, matching, and analogies. Some tests employ context clue strategies such as synonyms and antonyms and general meaning. Critical thinking skills are an important part of each test. (Answers to the Self-Tests appear in the Instructor's Manual.)

- **Word Wise:** Following the Self-Tests is the Word Wise section that teaches a variety of skills that are helpful to vocabulary acquisition. There are seven types of activities: Internet Activities, A Different Approach, Context Clue Mini-Lessons, Interesting Etymologies, Collocations, Word Pairs, and Connotations and Denotations. Each activity is explained in the Getting Started section. By doing these activities and reading more about how words are used, students will get additional practice and insight into the words they are learning.

- **Interactive Exercise:** Following the Word Wise section is an Interactive Exercise, which asks the student to begin actively using the vocabulary words. The exercises may include writing, making lists, or answering questions. The Interactive Exercises give students the chance to really think about the meanings of the words, but, more importantly, they encourage students to begin using the words actively. Some instructors like to have their students do the Interactive Exercise in small groups (or pairs) and then have the groups share their responses with the whole class. (See the Instructor's Manual for more ideas on collaborative activities.)

- **Hint, Word Part Reminder, or Conversation Starters:** Each chapter includes a Hint, a Word Part Reminder, or Conversation Starters. The Hints cover tips for developing vocabulary, reading, or study skills; the Hints are brief and practical, and students will be able to make use of them in all of their college courses. The Word Part Reminders are short exercises that give students a chance to practice using a few of the word parts they have recently learned. The Conversation Starters are questions that ask students to use the words while talking with each other. The goal of the Conversation Starters is to get students using the words in daily life.

- **Word List:** Following the Hint, Word Part Reminder, or Conversation Starter is a list of the vocabulary words with a pronunciation guide, the part of speech, and a brief definition for each. I wrote these definitions with the idea of keeping them simple and non-technical. Some vocabulary texts provide complicated dictionary definitions that include words students do not know; I've tried to make the definitions as friendly and as useful as possible.

- **Words to Watch:** This section asks students to pick 3–5 words they may be having trouble with and to write their own sentences using the words. This section is an additional chance for students to grasp the meaning of a few words that may be difficult for them.

Additional Features

In addition to the thematic vocabulary chapters, *Active Vocabulary* includes a Getting Started chapter, three Word Parts Chapters, five Review Chapters, a Glossary, a Flash Card section, a Word List, and a Pronunciation section.

- **Getting Started:** *Active Vocabulary* begins with an introductory chapter to familiarize students with some of the tools of vocabulary acquisition. The "Parts of Speech" section gives sample words and sentences for the eight parts of speech. "Using the Dictionary" dissects a sample dictionary entry and provides an exercise for using guide words. "Completing Analogies" explains how analogies work, provides sample analogies, and gives students analogy exercises to complete. This section will prepare students for the analogy Self-Tests contained in several chapters of the text. The "Benefits of Flash Cards" section encourages students to make flash cards beginning with Chapter 1. The section explains the advantages of using flash cards and makes students aware of the "Create Your Own Flash Cards" section at the end of the text. The "Word Wise Features" section provides background information for the various Word Wise activities.

- **Word Parts:** The three Word Parts Chapters introduce prefixes, roots, and suffixes used throughout the book. Students learn the meanings of these forms, and sample words illustrate the forms. Self-Tests in each Word Parts Chapter give students the opportunity to practice using the word parts.

- **Review Chapters:** Five Review Chapters focus on the preceding three or four chapters. They divide the words into different activity groups and test students' cumulative knowledge. The words appear in artistic, test, written, puzzle, and collaborative formats. These repeated and varied exposures increase the likelihood that the students will remember the words, not just for one chapter or test, but for life.

- **Glossary:** The Glossary is new to this edition. It lists all the vocabulary words along with the part of speech and the definitions given in each chapter. Students may find it handy to refer to the Glossary when reviewing words from several chapters.

- **Create Your Own Flash Cards:** The "Create Your Own Flash Cards" section teaches students how to make and use flash cards. Students can use the cards for self-study. Additionally, instructors can use them for the supplemental activities and games that are provided in the Instructor's Manual. Flash card templates are located in the back of the text. Students can photocopy the blank pages if they want to use this format, or they can use index cards as described in the flash card directions.

- **Pronunciation Key:** On the inside front cover is a pronunciation key to help students understand the pronunciation symbols used in this text. The inside front cover also offers some additional guidelines on pronunciation issues.

- **Word List:** The inside back cover features a list of all the vocabulary words and the page numbers on which the definitions are given. A list of the word parts from the Word Parts Chapters is also included on the inside back cover with page references.

Features New to this Edition

This fourth edition has several new features in response to instructor comments. The new materials and organization of the book have been employed to make the text more appealing to students and easier for instructors to use.

- **Refined In-Chapter Organization:** All of the analogy Self-Tests have been moved to the third exercise in a chapter to allow students more time to work with the words before they encounter this more challenging activity.

- **Added Content:** Two additional Review Chapters have been added to the text to help students reinforce and more quickly assess their learning of the words. The final activity in the Review Chapters, Mix It Up, has two new collaborative activities in addition to the ones from the previous edition. These activities give students a chance to use other skills such as memorization, writing, musical awareness, and acting with and without speaking. Word Part Reminders and Conversation Starters have been interspersed with the Hints as additional ways to help students remember the vocabulary words. A Glossary has been added to aid instructors and students in quickly finding a definition they want to review.

- **New Readings:** About a third of the chapters have new readings in either topics or formats more likely to appeal to students. Some of the readings have been lengthened to give students more reading practice and to provide more background information on the topic. Additionally, new words have been added to several chapters.

- **Updated Design:** New photographs have been added to some of the readings for more visually friendly chapters. The artwork has been redone in some chapters for a more sophisticated look. And the layout of the text has been redesigned for simplicity and freshness.

- **New Web Site:** The CD-ROM that formally accompanied *Active Vocabulary* has been transferred to the Internet to allow for easier student access and timelier updating of the exercises.

The Teaching and Learning Package

Each component of the teaching and learning package for *Active Vocabulary* has been carefully crafted to maximize the main text's value.

- **Instructor's Manual and Test Bank (ISBN 0-205-63279-3):** The Instructor's Manual and Test Bank, which is almost as long as the main text, includes options for additional Collaborative Activities and games. The collaborative section explains ways students can share their work on the Interactive Exercises in pairs, in small groups, or with the whole class. Ideas for other collaborative activities using different learning styles are also offered. The games section presents games that can be used with individual chapters or for review of several chapters. Some of the games are individual; others are full-class activities. Some games have winners, and some are just for fun. The games may involve acting, drawing, or writing. The Collaborative Activities and games give students the opportunity to use the words in conversational settings and a chance to work with others.

    The Test Bank, formatted for easy copying, includes two to three tests for each chapter as well as combined tests of two chapters. There are also Mastery Tests to accompany the Review Chapters and full-book Mastery Tests that can be used as final exams.

- *Active Vocabulary* **Web Site:** In the computer age, many students enjoy learning via computers. Available with this text is access to the *Active Vocabulary* Web site, which features additional exercises and tests that provide for even more interaction between the students and the words. The Web site has an audio component that allows students to hear each chapter's thematic reading and the pronunciation of each word as often as they choose. Students are often reluctant to use the new words they learn because they aren't sure how to pronounce them. The pronunciation guides in each chapter do help to address this fear, but actually hearing the words spoken will give students greater confidence in using the words. Contact your Longman publishing representative for information on how to access the Web site.

For Additional Reading and Reference

The Longman Basic Skills Package

In addition to the book-specific supplements discussed above, many other skills-based supplements are available for both instructors and students. All of these supplements are available either at no additional cost or at greatly reduced prices.

- **The Dictionary Deal.** Two dictionaries can be shrink-wrapped with *Active Vocabulary* at a nominal fee. *The New American Webster Handy College Dictionary* is a paperback reference text with more than 100,000 entries. *Merriam-Webster's Collegiate Dictionary,* eleventh edition, is a hardback reference with a citation file of more than 14.5 million examples of English words drawn from actual use. For more information on how to shrink-wrap a dictionary with your text, please contact your Longman publishing representative.

- **Longman Vocabulary Web Site.** For additional vocabulary-related resources, visit our free vocabulary Web site at **http://www.ablongman.com/vocabulary**.

- **MyReadingLab (www.myreadinglab.com).** The lab, where better reading skills are within reach, is a collection of reading, vocabulary, and study skills activities consolidated into a central suite. At the heart of MyReadingLab is the interactive tutorial system Reading Road Trip, the most widely used reading tutorial software. Reading Road Trip takes students on a tour of sixteen landmarks in different cities throughout the United States; at each attraction students learn and practice a different reading skill while absorbing the local color. MyReadingLab will also include access to the Longman Vocabulary Web site, Pearson Study Skills Web site, and Research Navigator.

To the Student

This book is designed to make learning vocabulary fun. You will increase the benefits of this book if you keep a few points in mind:

1. **Interact with the words.** Each chapter contains eight exposures to a word, and your instructor may introduce one or two additional activities. If you're careful in your reading and thorough in doing the activities for each chapter, learning the words will be fun and easy.

2. **Appreciate the importance of words.** The words for the readings were picked from popular magazines and newspapers, novels, lists of words likely to appear on standardized tests (such as SAT and GRE), and textbooks from a variety of academic disciplines. These are words you will encounter in everyday life and in the classroom. Learning these words will help you be a more informed citizen and make your academic life much richer. Even if you don't currently have an interest in one of the readings, keep an open mind: the words may appear in the article you read in tomorrow's newspaper or on an exam in one of next semester's classes. The readings also come in different formats as a reminder that you can learn new vocabulary anywhere—from the newspaper to journal entries.

3. **Find your preferred learning style.** This book aims to provide exercises for all types of learners—visual, aural, and interpersonal. But only you can say which learning style works best for you. See which activities (drawings, acting, matching, completing stories) you like most, and replicate those activities when they aren't part of the chapter.

4. **Value critical thinking.** The variety of exercise formats you will find in the following pages make the book fun to work with and build a range of critical thinking skills. For example, the analogies will help you see relationships between words, the fill-in-the-blank formats will aid you in learning to put words into context, and the true/false Self-Tests will focus your attention on whether words are used correctly in a sentence. Each type of activity will develop your critical thinking skills while building your vocabulary.

5. **Remember that learning is fun.** Don't make a chore out of learning new words, or any other new skill for that matter. If you enjoy what you're doing, you're more likely to welcome the information and to retain it.

Enjoy your journey through *Active Vocabulary!*

—AMY E. OLSEN

Access to the *Active Vocabulary* Web Site

The Web site features additional exercises and tests for more interaction between you and the words. The Web site also has an audio component that allows you to hear each chapter's thematic reading and the pronunciation of each word as often as you choose. Ask your instructor how to access the Web site.

Acknowledgments

I want to thank the following reviewers for their helpful suggestions as the fourth edition took shape: Susan Paterson, Asheville-Buncombe Technical Community College; Marilee McGowan, Oakton Community College; Barbara Sussman, Miami Dade College; Nancy Fagel, Miami Dade College; Marian Dillahunt, Vance Granville Community College; Mary Likely, Nassau Community College; and Dr. Gary Kay, Broward Community College.

Additionally, I want to thank Kate Edwards, Acquisitions Editor of Reading and Study Skills at Pearson Longman and Lindsey Allen, Editorial Assistant, for their help in organizing this edition. Thanks also to the Supplement, Marketing, and Production departments of Pearson Longman for their efforts on various aspects of the book. I am grateful to my colleagues for their support and enlightening discussions. I warmly thank my family for their encouragement now and over the years. And I shower my husband with gratitude for giving up some of his computer time while I spent many long hours on it during the revision process.

I am pleased that this new edition maintains the goal of this series to combine traditional and innovative approaches to vocabulary study. I am proud to present the fourth edition of *Active Vocabulary,* a book that makes learning vocabulary fun and meaningful.

—AMY E. OLSEN

Also Available

Book 1 of the Vocabulary Series:
Interactive Vocabulary: General Words, by Amy E. Olsen

Book 3 of the Vocabulary Series:
Academic Vocabulary: Academic Words, by Amy E. Olsen

Word List

PART I General Words

Getting Started

page 30

page 40

page 66

Getting Started

Parts of Speech

There are eight parts of speech. A word's part of speech is based on how the word is used in a sentence. Words can, therefore, be more than one part of speech. For an example, note how the word *punch* is used below.

nouns: (n.) name a person, place, or thing

> EXAMPLES: Ms. Lopez, New Orleans, lamp, warmth

> *Ms. Lopez* enjoyed her *trip* to *New Orleans* where she bought a beautiful *lamp*. The *warmth* of the *sun* filled *Claire* with *happiness*. I drank five *cups* of the orange *punch*.

pronouns: (pron.) take the place of a noun

> EXAMPLES: I, me, you, she, he, it, her, we, they, my, which, that, anybody, everybody

> *Everybody* liked the music at the party. *It* was the kind that made people want to dance. *They* bought a new car, *which* hurt their bank account.

verbs: (v.) express an action or state of being

> EXAMPLES: enjoy, run, think, read, dance, am, is, are, was, were

> Lily *read* an interesting book yesterday. I *am* tired. He *is* an excellent student. She *punched* the bully.

adjectives: (adj.) modify (describe or explain) a noun or pronoun

> EXAMPLES: pretty, old, two, expensive, red, small

> The *old* car was covered with *red* paint on *one* side. The *two* women met for lunch at an *expensive* restaurant. The *punch* bowl was *empty* soon after Uncle Al got to the party.

adverbs: (adv.) modify a verb, an adjective, or another adverb

> EXAMPLES: very, shortly, first, too, soon, quickly, finally, furthermore, however

> We will meet *shortly* after one o'clock. The *very* pretty dress sold *quickly*. I liked her; *however*, there was something strange about her.

prepositions: (prep.) are placed before a noun or pronoun to create a phrase that relates to other parts of the sentence

> EXAMPLES: after, around, at, before, by, from, in, into, of, off, on, through, to, up, with

> He told me to be *at* his house *in* the afternoon. You must go *through* all the steps to do the job.

conjunctions: (conj.) join words or other sentence elements and show a relationship between the connected items

> EXAMPLES: and, but, or, nor, for, so, yet, after, although, because, if, since, than, when

> I went to the movies, *and* I went to dinner on Tuesday. I will not go to the party this weekend *because* I have to study. I don't want to hear your reasons *or* excuses.

interjections: (interj.) show surprise or emotion

> EXAMPLES: oh, hey, wow, ah, ouch

> I forgot to do my homework! *Wow,* I got an A on the test!

1

Using the Dictionary

There will be times when you need to use a dictionary for one of its many features; becoming familiar with dictionary **entries** will make using a dictionary more enjoyable. The words in a dictionary are arranged alphabetically. The words on a given page are signaled by **guide words** at the top of the page. If the word you are looking for comes alphabetically between these two words, then your word is on that page. When using online dictionaries, you will simply type in the word you are looking for, so guide words will not be important, but the other features of an entry remain the same.

1436 · **wing tip • wintry** ◄— Guide words

wing tip *n* (ca. 1908) **1 a** : the edge or outer margin of a bird's wing **b** *usu* **wingtip** : the outer end of an airplane wing **2** : a toe cap having a point that extends back toward the throat of the shoe and curving sides that extend toward the shank **3** : a shoe having a wing tip

¹**wink** \'wiŋk\ *vb* [ME, fr. OE *wincian;* akin to OHG *winchan* to stagger, wink and perh. to L *vacillare* to sway, Skt *vañcati* he goes crookedly] *vi* (bef. 12c) **1** : to shut one eye briefly as a signal or in teasing **2** : to close and open the eyelids quickly **3** : to avoid seeing or noting something — usu. used with *at* **4** : to gleam or flash intermittently: TWINKLE <her glasses ~*ing* in the sunlight — Harper Lee> **5 a** : to come to an end — usu. used with *out* **b** : to stop shining — usu. used with *out* **6** : to signal a message with a light ~ *vt* **1** : to cause to open and shut **2** : to affect or influence by or as if by blinking the eyes

²**wink** *n* (14c) **1** : a brief period of sleep : NAP <catching a ~> **2 a** : a hint or sign given by winking **b** : an act of winking **3** : the time of a wink: INSTANT <quick as a ~> **4** : a flicker of the eyelids: BLINK

wink·er \'wiŋ-kər\ *n* (1549) **1** : one that winks **2** : a horse's blinder

¹**win·kle** \'wiŋ-kəl\ *n* [by shortening] (1585) : ²PERIWINKLE

²**winkle** *vi* **win·kled; win·kling** \-k(ə-)liŋ\ [freq. of *wink*] (1791): TWINKLE

³**winkle** *vt* **win·kled; win·kling** \-k(ə-)liŋ\ [¹*winkle;* fr. the process of extracting a winkle from its shell] (1918) **1** *chiefly Brit* : to displace, remove, or evict from a position — usu. used with *out* **2** *chiefly Brit* : to obtain or draw out by effort — usu. used with *out* <no attempt to ~ out why they do it — Joan Bakewell>

win·ner \'wi-nər\ *n* (14c) : one that wins: as **a** : one that is successful esp. through praise-worthy ability and hard work **b** : a victor esp. in games and sports **c** : one that wins admiration **d** : a shot in a court game that is not returned and that scores for the player making it

win·ter·ize \'win-tə-,rīz\ *vt* **-ized ; -iz·ing** (1934) : to make ready for winter or winter use and esp. resistant or proof against winter weather <~ a car> — **win·ter·i·za·tion** \,win-tə-rə-'zā-shən\ *n*

win·ter—kill \'win-tər-,kil\ *vt* (ca. 1806) : to kill (as a plant) by exposure to winter conditions ~ *vi* : to die as a result of exposure to winter conditions — **winterkill** *n*

win·ter·ly \'win-tər-lē\ *adj* (1559) : of, relating to, or occurring in winter . WINTRY

winter melon *n* (ca. 1900) **1** : any of several muskmelons (as a casaba or honeydew melon) that are fruits of a cultivated vine (*Cucumis melo indorus*) **2** : a large white-fleshed melon that is the fruit of an Asian vine (*Benincasa hispida*) and is used esp. in Chinese cooking

winter quarters *n pl but sing or pl in constr* (1641) : a winter residence or station (as of a military unit or a circus)

winter savory *n* (1597) : a perennial European mint (*Satureja montana*) with leaves used for seasoning — compare SUMMER SAVORY

winter squash *n* (1775) : any of various hard-shelled squashes that belong to cultivars derived from several species (esp. *Cucurbita maxima, C. moschata,* and *C. pepo*) and that can be stored for several months

win·ter·tide \'win-tər-,tīd\ *n* (bef. 12c) : WINTERTIME

win·ter·time \-,tīm\ *n* (14c) : the season of winter

win through *vi* (1644) : to survive difficulties and reach a desired or satisfactory end <*win through* to a better life beyond — B. F. Reilly>

win·tle \'wi-nᵊl, 'win-tᵊl\ *vi* **win·tled; win·tling** \'win(t)-liŋ; 'wi-nᵊl-iŋ, 'win-tᵊl-\ [perh. fr. D dial. *windtelen* to reel] (1786) **1** *Scot* : STAGGER, REEL **2** *Scot* : WRIGGLE

win·try \'win-trē\ *also* **win·tery** \'win-t(ə-)rē\ *adj* **win·tri·er; -est** (bef. 12c) **1** : of, relating to, or characteristic of winter **2 a** : weathered by or as if by winter : AGED, HOARY **b** : CHEERLESS, CHILLING <a ~ greeting> — **win·tri·ness** \'win-trē-nəs\ *n*

Entry

Most dictionaries contain the following information in an entry:

- The **pronunciation**—symbols show how a word should be spoken, including how the word is divided into syllables and where the stress should be placed on a word. The Pronunciation Key for this book is located on the inside front cover. The key shows the symbols used to indicate the sound of a word. Every dictionary has a pronunciation method, and a pronunciation key or guide is usually found in the front pages, with a partial key at the bottom of each page. The differences in the pronunciation systems used by dictionaries are usually slight.
- The **part of speech**—usually abbreviated, such as *n.* for noun, *v.* for verb, and *adj.* for adjective. A key to these abbreviations and others is usually found in the front of the dictionary.
- The **definition**—usually the most common meaning is listed first followed by other meanings.
- An **example of the word in a sentence**—the sentence is usually in italics and follows each meaning.
- **Synonyms** and **antonyms**—*synonyms* are words with similar meanings, and *antonyms* are words with opposite meanings. (You should also consider owning a **thesaurus**, a book that lists synonyms and antonyms.)
- The **etymology**—the history of a word, usually including the language(s) it came from.
- The **spelling of different forms** of the word—these forms may include unusual plurals and verb tenses (especially irregular forms).

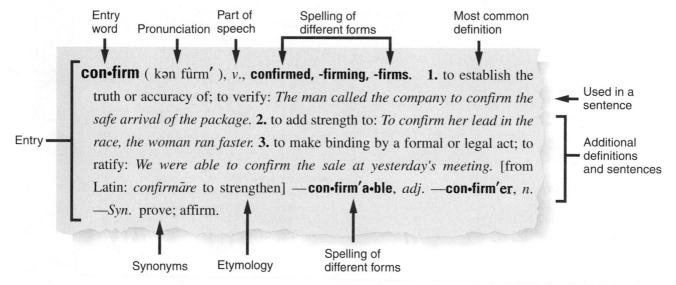

Despite the popularity of online dictionaries, it can still be handy to own a paper version. When choosing a dictionary, take the time to look at different dictionaries to see what appeals to you. Dictionaries come in several sizes and are made for different purposes. First read some of the entries to see if the definitions make sense to you. See which of the features above are used in the dictionary. Is it important to you to be able to study the etymology of a word? Would you like sample sentences? Some dictionaries have illustrations in the margins. Decide if that is a feature you would use. Check to see if the print is large enough for you to read easily.

Decide on how you will use this dictionary. Do you want a paperback dictionary to put in your backpack? Or is this going to be the dictionary for your desk and a large hardback version would be the better choice? Several disciplines have specialized dictionaries with meanings that apply to those fields, such as law or medicine. There are also bilingual dictionaries, such as French/English or Spanish/English, that can be helpful for school or travel. Take time in picking out your dictionary because a good dictionary will be a companion for years to come. A few dictionaries to consider are *Merriam-Webster's Collegiate Dictionary, The American Heritage Dictionary, The Random House College Dictionary,* and *The Oxford Dictionary.*

In general, when you are reading, try to use context clues, the words around the word you don't know, to first figure out the meaning of a word, but if you are still in doubt, don't hesitate to refer to a dictionary for the exact definition. Don't forget that dictionaries also contain more than definitions and are an essential reference source for any student.

Using Guide Words

Use the sample guide words to determine on which page each of the ten words will be found. Write the page number next to the entry word.

Page	Guide Words
157	bone/boo
159	boot/born
435	endemic/endorse
654	humanist/humongous
655	humor/hunter
975	pamphlet/pandemonium
976	pander/pant
1480	velvet/venom

Example: _654_ humdinger

_____ 1. panorama

_____ 2. pancake

_____ 3. bonus

_____ 4. Venice

_____ 5. endless

_____ 6. hunch

_____ 7. border

_____ 8. panic

_____ 9. hummingbird

_____ 10. humdrum

Entry Identification

Label the parts of the following entry.

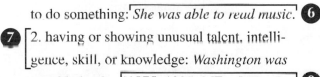

a•ble (ā′ bəl) *adj.* **a•bler, a•blest.** 1. having the necessary power, skill, or qualifications to do something: *She was able to read music.* 2. having or showing unusual talent, intelligence, skill, or knowledge: *Washington was an able leader.* [1275–1325; ME < MF < L *habilis* easy to handle, adaptable=*hab(ēre)* to have, hold + *ilis* –ile] *Syn.* apt, talented.

1. _____

2. _____

3. _____

4. _____

5. _____

6. _____

7. _____

8. _____

9. _____

Completing Analogies

An **analogy** shows a relationship between words. Working with analogies helps one to see connections between items, which is a crucial critical thinking skill. Analogies are written as follows: big : large :: fast : quick. The colon (:) means *is to*. The analogy reads big *is to* large as fast *is to* quick. To complete analogies

1. find a relationship between the first pair of words
2. look for a similar relationship in another set of words

In the example above, *big* and *large* have similar meanings; they are synonyms. *Fast* and *quick* also have similar meanings, so the relationship between the four words uses synonyms.
    Common relationships used in analogies (with examples) include

synonyms (trip : journey)   grammatical structure (shaking : shivering)

antonyms (real : fake)   cause and effect (step in a puddle : get wet)

examples (strawberry : fruit)   sequences (turn on car : drive)

part to a whole (handle : cup)   an object to a user or its use (spatula : chef)

Analogies in this book come in matching and fill-in-the-blank forms. Try the following analogies for practice.

Matching

1. old : young ::   _____   a. preface : book

2. clip coupons : go shopping ::   _____   b. put on shoes : take a walk

3. peel : banana ::   _____   c. low wages : strike

4. no rain : drought ::   _____   d. rested : tired

Fill-in-the-Blank

writer	passion	abduct	sadly

5. frozen : chilled :: kidnap : _____

6. interrupting : rude :: embracing : _____

7. slow : slowly :: sad : _____

8. baton : conductor :: computer : _____

Answers

1. To figure out this analogy, first one needs to see that *old* and *young* are opposites, or **antonyms**. Next look at the choices and see if another pair of words are antonyms, and, yes, *rested* and *tired* are opposites. The answer is d.

2. A person would *clip coupons* and then *go shopping,* so there is a **sequence** of events. Of the choices, one would *put on shoes* and then *take a walk,* another sequence. The answer is b.

3. A *peel* is a part of a *banana,* while a *preface* is part of a *book,* so the connection is **part to a whole**. The answer is a.

4. When an area gets *no rain,* it can lead to a *drought,* and when people get paid *low wages,* they can go on *strike.* The connection among these pairs is **cause and effect**. The answer is c.

5. *Frozen* and *chilled* have similar meanings; they are **synonyms**. To solve the analogy, pick a word that has a similar meaning to *kidnap,* which would be *abduct.*

6. *Interrupting* a person is **an example** of a *rude* behavior. *Embracing* is an example of another type of behavior; in this case, it fits as an example of *passion.*

7. *Slow* is an adjective, and *slowly* is an adverb; *sad* is an adjective, and *sadly* is an adverb. This analogy works by using the same **grammatical structure** between the words.

8. A *baton* is used by a *conductor.* Who uses a *computer?* Among the choices, *writer* obviously fits. The relationship here is **object to user**.

Sometimes you may come up with a relationship between the first two words that makes sense but doesn't fit any of the choices. Look at the choices and the two words again to see if you can find a way any four words fit together. Also do any obvious matches first, and with fewer choices it will be easier to spot the harder connections. Doing analogies can be fun as you begin to make clever connections and see word relationships in new ways. Finding word connections will help your brain make other connections in areas as diverse as writing essays, doing math problems, and arranging travel plans. Analogies are just another way to exercise your thinking skills.

Try a few more analogies, and check your answers on page 12 to see how you did.

Matching

1. button : shirt ::   _____   a. broom : janitor

2. map : traveler ::   _____   b. drawer : desk

3. calm : tranquil ::   _____   c. stayed up late : exhausted

4. watched a comedy : laughed ::   _____   d. wise : smart

Fill-in-the-Blank

huge	beverage	warmth	sleep

5. make dinner : eat :: put on pajamas : _____

6. dull : bright :: tiny : _____

7. trunk : storage :: coat : _____

8. the Nile : a river :: iced tea : _____

Benefits of Flash Cards

There are several benefits to using flash cards to help you study vocabulary words.

Making the Cards   The first benefit comes from just making the cards. When you make a card, you will practice writing the word and its definition. You may also write a sentence using the word, record its part of speech, or draw a picture of the word. See the section "Create Your Own Flash Cards" on page 172 at the back of this book for ideas on how to make flash cards. Creating the cards allows for a personal experience with the words, which makes learning the words easier.

Working with Others   Another benefit is that using the cards can lead to collaborative activities. When you ask a friend, family member, or classmate to quiz you on the words, you get the chance to work with someone else, which many people enjoy. You may even establish a study group with the friends you find from quizzing each other on your flash cards.

Evaluating Your Learning   A third benefit is that the cards serve as pre-tests that let you evaluate how well you know a word. When a friend quizzes you, ask him or her to go over the words you miss several times. As the stack of flash cards with words you don't know gets smaller, you know that the words are becoming part of your vocabulary. You know that you are prepared to face a word on a quiz or test when you can correctly give the definition several times.

Making and using the flash cards should be fun. Enjoy the process of learning new words. Turn to the back of the book now to review the directions for creating flash cards, and you will be ready to make cards beginning with Chapter 1. You can use the templates provided at the end of the book to get started.

Word Wise Features

The Word Wise boxes share information on different areas related to vocabulary. There are seven types of features.

Internet Activity   suggests ways to use technology to enhance your learning experience.

A Different Approach   presents activities that you can do alone or collaboratively that allow you to interact with the vocabulary words using diverse methods, such as art, creative writing, and word groups. These other techniques can help to stimulate your mind and organize the vocabulary you are learning.

Context Clue Mini-Lessons   provide different types of context-clue situations and give you the opportunity to practice using each type. *Context* means the words surrounding a specific word that give clues to that word's meaning. When you encounter a word whose meaning you don't know, keep reading the passage, looking for clues to help you figure out the meaning. These clues might be in the same sentence as the unknown words or in a sentence that comes before or after the word. Look for these types of clues in a passage:

Synonyms—words that have a similar meaning to the unknown word

Antonyms—words that mean the opposite of the unknown word

Examples—a list of items that explain the unknown word

General meaning—the meaning of the sentence or passage as a whole that could clarify the meaning of the unknown word

Each type of context clue has a mini-lesson, and a final lesson combines the methods. You will not find a context clue every time you encounter a word you don't know, but being aware of context clues will help you determine the meaning of many new words and make reading more enjoyable.

Interesting Etymologies presents notable word histories. Some of the histories use the word parts presented in the three Word Parts chapters of the text. Learning the history of a word can help you to remember its meaning.

Collocations show ways words are used together. The groupings can come in several forms, such as a verb with a noun (*commit* a *crime*), an adjective with a noun (*handsome stranger*), or a verb with a preposition (*come over*). Learning collocations will help you understand common ways to use the words you are studying. Sentences with the collocations in italics for some of the vocabulary words in this text are spread throughout the chapters. To become more familiar with collocations, look and listen for other repeated word combinations in the materials you read, in the phrases people use when speaking, and as you do the Self-Tests in this book.

Word Pairs illustrate how some words are often used near each other. Learning word pairs can help you to better remember both words. Some words are pairs because the items they represent are often used together, such as peanut butter and jelly. Other word pairs are opposites that are often found together when describing objects, actions, or people (such as "My friends are as different as night and day"). Word pairs are presented in several chapters with sample sentences to show how the words can be used near each other.

Connotations and Denotations examine reactions to a word. A **denotation** is "the explicit or direct meaning of a word." This is the kind of definition you would find in the dictionary. A **connotation** is "the suggestive or associative meaning of a word beyond its literal definition." This is the emotional response you have to a word. (A mnemonic device for remembering the difference between the two is that denotation begins with a "d," and it is the dictionary or direct meaning, both beginning with a "d").

It is important to realize that words have two kinds of meanings because careful writers use both kinds. You, as a writer and reader, want to make sure you are clearly expressing your point and understanding another writer's ideas by recognizing how words are used. Some connotations are personal reactions. For example, *seclusion* in Chapter 7 means "solitude; a sheltered place." Depending on your personality or current living conditions, you might picture *seclusion* as a wonderful chance to be alone and relax without all the chaos surrounding you, or if you hate being by yourself, you may envision it as a kind of torture separating you from friends and family. Other connotations have broader emotional responses. If you wanted to describe a thin person, you could use the words *slender* or *scrawny*. What do you picture in your mind for each word? Talk to your classmates about their images. Are they similar? Some words have positive connotations that people feel good about, and other words have negative connotations that turn people off. Not all words have strong connotations. For most people a pencil is a pencil, and there isn't much to get excited about. But other words can bring out strong feelings, such as *frugal*. The Connotation and Denotation lessons look at some of the vocabulary words in this text and the differences in their meanings.

The Classroom

Learning New Skills

Wyckoff College

Angie Nelson	**Study Skills 1A**	**Fall 2009**
Office: #46	**Phone: 555-6330**	**Office hours: TBA**

Syllabus

5 Welcome to an exciting semester! In this course, you will learn how to improve your reading skills, take effective notes, efficiently use your time, and make your college experience more rewarding. For many students, studying becomes the **bane** of their existence. They would rather socialize with friends, play sports, or watch television. But studying does not have to ruin your fun. You can enjoy your classes and your other activities using the tools that will be presented in this course.

Objectives: to improve your reading, writing, listening, and critical thinking skills so that you can successfully
10 transfer these skills to your other college courses.

Required Texts: Reading Now. 1st ed.
                   Active Vocabulary. 4th ed.

Required Materials: a **durable** notebook (one that will last the entire semester), 8 1/2" x 11" loose-leaf notebook paper, a stapler, a black pen, a #2 pencil, and a collegiate dictionary such as The American Heritage Dictionary or
15 Merriam-Webster's Collegiate Dictionary.

Absences: I reserve the right to drop a student after three absences. Missing class can significantly influence your learning and your grade. Your presence in the classroom **indicates** your readiness to learn.

Assignments: The assignments for this class will **comprise** weekly reading quizzes, a midterm, an in-class essay, a final, and a variety of homework projects. The weekly quizzes will test your ability to comprehend what you read
20 and your skill in using the **terminology** introduced in the readings. Increasing your vocabulary will make reading easier and more rewarding. The midterm and final will contain short answer and multiple-choice questions.

Homework	Weekly	15%
Reading quizzes	Every Monday	20%
Midterm exam	Week 8	20%
In-class essay	Week 13	20%
Final exam	Week 16	25%

Tips to get you started:

• Take notes each class. Don't **undermine** your education by ignoring this vital part of studying. Taking notes will help you remember information, and reviewing the notes throughout the term will reinforce your learning.

30 • Come to class prepared: bring a focused mind, completed assignments, and required materials.

• Become a **zealous** student. Students who are enthusiastic about a subject do better. **Apathy** is the enemy of education. If you lack interest in a subject, search for a way to make it meaningful to you.

• Find a comfortable and quiet place to study.

• Create a support group of classmates, friends, and family.

35 • Learn to handle setbacks. Don't needlessly **berate** yourself if you don't do well on a quiz or other assignment. Instead of criticizing yourself to the point where you want to give up, look at what went wrong. Maybe you needed to study more or you read a question too fast. Work to do better next time.

The rest of the syllabus outlines the readings and due dates of the homework assignments. Follow the calendar to keep up with the work. I look forward to a fun and enriching semester for all of us.

Predicting

For each set, write the definition on the line next to the word to which it belongs. If you are unsure, return to the reading on page 10, and underline any context clues you find. After you've made your predictions, check your answers against the Word List on page 15. Place a checkmark in the box next to each word whose definition you missed. These are the words you'll want to study closely.

Set One

something that ruins or spoils	to be composed of	reveals
lasting	an outline	

☐ 1. **syllabus** (line 3) _____

☐ 2. **bane** (line 6) _____

☐ 3. **durable** (line 13) _____

☐ 4. **indicates** (line 17) _____

☐ 5. **comprise** (line 18) _____

Set Two

enthusiastic	to weaken or damage	to criticize	lack of interest
the study of terms for particular subjects			

☐ 6. **terminology** (line 20) _____

☐ 7. **undermine** (line 28) _____

☐ 8. **zealous** (line 31) _____

☐ 9. **apathy** (line 31) _____

☐ 10. **berate** (line 35) _____

Self-Tests

1 Match each term with its synonym in Set One and its antonym in Set Two.

SYNONYMS

Set One

_____ 1. terminology   a. outline

_____ 2. bane   b. reveal

_____ 3. comprise   c. terms

_____ 4. syllabus   d. include

_____ 5. indicate   e. irritation

ANTONYMS

_____ 6. undermine   f. bored

_____ 7. durable   g. praise

_____ 8. berate   h. enthusiasm

_____ 9. apathy   i. temporary

_____10. zealous   j. strengthen

2 Circle the correct word to complete each sentence.

1. I hope my textbooks are (zealous, durable) because I am going to be using them a lot.

2. The 10th anniversary committee will (berate, comprise) students, faculty, staff, and administrators.

3. The teacher handed out the (bane, syllabus) on the first day of class.

4. My friend was jealous of my relationship, so he tried to (undermine, comprise) it by telling my girlfriend that I was seen kissing another woman.

5. I enjoy leading tours for children. They are so (durable, zealous); they want to see and do everything.

6. The (apathy, terminology) for my chemistry class is all so new to me. I have had to really study the vocabulary to make sure I am doing the right things in the lab.

7. All the phone calls this week (indicate, comprise) that we will have a large turnout for the book club meeting on Friday.

8. Weeds are the (bane, terminology) of my life as a gardener.

9. When I was young, my mother always had to (berate, undermine) me to clean my room; now that I have my own apartment, I want to keep it clean.

10. The crowd's (syllabus, apathy) did not inspire the players to try harder once they were behind by twenty points.

Answers to the analogies practice in the Getting Started section on page 7:
1. b   2. a   3. d   4. c   5. sleep   6. huge   7. warmth   8. beverage

3 Complete the sentences using the vocabulary words. Use each word once.

1. I was worried about my cousin's _____; she did not feel like going out for two months after her dog died.

2. I refer to the _____ for my psychology class every Friday to know what to read for the weekend.

3. The teacher had to _____ several students when they failed to do their homework two class sessions in a row.

4. The bank highlighted certain lines to _____ where I needed to sign my loan papers.

5. Once I learned the _____ at my new job, it was much easier to understand my boss when she asked me to do something.

6. My day will mainly _____ errands, but I hope to take at least an hour to walk in the park.

7. The _____ student went to the library to read more about advertising after learning some techniques in his marketing class.

8. The table in the dining room has been in my family for five hundred years. It certainly has proved to be _____.

9. A couple bad test results can _____ a student's confidence and lead to further poor performances.

10. The constant work on her neighbor's house was a _____ on Martha's existence; all she wanted was some peace and quiet.

Word Wise

Context Clue Mini-Lesson 1

Context clues can come in several forms. See page 8 for more information on the various types of context clues. The mini-lessons spread throughout this text will give you a chance to practice looking for context clues by focusing on specific types of clues. This lesson features synonyms—words that have a similar meaning to the unknown word. In the paragraph below, circle the synonyms you find for the underlined words and write them on the lines that follow the paragraph.

I was having a good time at the party chatting with old friends and meeting new people. I met one affable man who had me laughing in seconds. He was so friendly that I felt like I had known him for years. Unfortunately, later in the evening he began to chastise me for eating cookies. He said he was scolding me because he cared about my health, but I knew a couple cookies weren't going to hurt me. I wasn't going to be compliant, and I told him I was not the obedient type who did whatever people told her. He got angry and began yelling at me. My elation in meeting him quickly disappeared; the joy I had felt in first talking to him became a distant memory.

The Synonym

1. Affable _____

2. Chastise _____

3. Compliant _____

4. Elation _____

Interactive Exercise

Practice using the vocabulary words by answering the following questions related to education.

1. What could a durable notebook be made of?

   _____

2. How can you indicate your interest in a course to your instructor?

   _____

   _____

3. What are two items that are usually mentioned on a syllabus?

   _____

   _____

4. How can you undermine your study habits to become a bad student?

   _____

   _____

5. What should you do instead of berate yourself if you don't do well on a test or paper?

   _____

   _____

6. What are two subjects that you are most zealous about?

   _____

7. What are three activities that comprise your average school day?

   _____

   _____

8. What are two causes that can contribute to student apathy?

   _____

9. What has been a bane to your schooling experience?

   _____

   _____

10. What are three subjects that you would expect to have a lot of terminology that most people would not be familiar with?

   _____

   _____

HINT

Flash Cards

Flash cards are a great way to study vocabulary. Turn to the "Create Your Own Flash Cards" section at the end of this book to read about ways to make and use flash cards. Remember to carry your flash cards with you and study for at least a few minutes each day. Also ask friends and family members to quiz you using the flash cards.

Word List

apathy
[ap′ ə thē]
  n. lack of interest; absence or suppression of emotion or excitement

bane
[bān]
  n. 1. something that ruins or spoils; irritation
    2. death or destruction
    3. a deadly poison

berate
[bi rāt′]
  v. to scold harshly; to criticize

comprise
[kəm prīz′]
  v. 1. to consist of; to be composed of
    2. to include; to contain; to form

durable
[dûr′ ə bəl]
  adj. lasting; firm; permanent

indicate
[in′ di kāt′]
  v. 1. to be a sign of; to show the need for; to reveal
    2. to point out or point to

syllabus
[sil′ ə bəs]
  n. an outline or other brief statement on the content of a course

terminology
[tûr′ mə nol′ ə jē]
  n. the study of terms for particular subjects; the terms belonging to a specialized subject; vocabulary

undermine
[un′ dər mīn′, un′dər mīn′]
  v. 1. to weaken or damage (such as health or morale) by small stages
    2. to weaken or cause to collapse by removing basic supports; to dig or tunnel beneath

zealous
[zel′ əs]
  adj. enthusiastic; eager; passionate

Words to Watch

Which words would you like to practice with a bit more? Pick 3–5 words to study, and list them below. Write the word and its definition, and compose your own sentence using the word correctly. This extra practice could be the final touch to learning a word.

	Word	Definition	Your Sentence
1.			
2.			
3.			
4.			
5.			

Relationships

Dealing with People

Answers from April

Dear April,
I just started college, and my roomate is destroying my **serenity**. I am usually a calm person, but my roommate's **dour** nature is upsetting me. Every time I come home, she has something depressing to say, and then I too feel gloomy. What can I do to cheer us both up?
Truly,
Desperate for help

Dear Desperate,
You cannot be **submissive** in this situation. Don't surrender to her unhappiness! You must **exemplify** the type of person you want your roommate to be. Show her how to be cheerful by being cheerful yourself. When she makes a depressing comment, respond with a positive view. Most people prefer to be around **amiable** people, and your roommate needs to see that. Take her out on the town, and let her see how people respond to a warm greeting and friendly face. If this plan doesn't work, start looking for a new roommate.

Dear April,
One of my new friends has recently disappointed me. I thought we had a real **affinity**. We have had great times going to movies and hiking on the weekends. However, in the last month, he hasn't been very **dependable** where money is concerned. He has borrowed money from me five times and never paid me back. I don't want to appear **mercenary**, but I am beginning to think he is just being my friend for financial reasons. The first loan was for five dollars, but last week he borrowed seventy dollars. Yesterday I hinted about my being short on cash hoping he would pay me back; instead, he suggested I get a second job. What should I do about this friendship?
Sincerely,
Looking for change

Dear Looking,
Quit being so **discreet**! Tell your friend he needs to pay you back immediately. If the direct method isn't **fruitful**, you will know that he is only interested in the friendship your wallet can provide. You may have to write off the loans as a learning experience. Good friends share similar interests, but they also respect each other by paying back money. It is time to find out if your friend has a bad memory or if he sees you as his personal ATM. Good luck!

5

10

15

20

25

30

35

40

45

50

55

16

Predicting |||||||||||||||||||||||||||||||||||||||||||||||||||||||||||||||||||||||||||||||||||||||||

For each set, write the definition on the line next to the word to which it belongs. If you are unsure, return to the reading on page 16, and underline any context clues you find. After you've made your predictions, check your answers against the Word List on page 21. Place a checkmark in the box next to each word whose definition you missed. These are the words you'll want to study closely.

Set One

gloomy	agreeable	passive	peacefulness	to represent

❑ 1. **serenity** (line 3) _____

❑ 2. **dour** (line 4) _____

❑ 3. **submissive** (line 12) _____

❑ 4. **exemplify** (line 14) _____

❑ 5. **amiable** (line 19) _____

Set Two

responsible	successful	liking	careful	greedy

❑ 6. **affinity** (line 28) _____

❑ 7. **dependable** (line 31) _____

❑ 8. **mercenary** (line 34) _____

❑ 9. **discreet** (line 46) _____

❑ 10. **fruitful** (line 48) _____

Self-Tests |||||||||||||||||||||||||||||||||||||||||||||||||||||||||||||||||||||||||||||||||||||||||||||||||||||

1 In each group, there are three synonyms and one antonym. Circle the antonym.

1. gloomy	happy	dour	forbidding
2. submissive	passive	obedient	aggressive
3. fondness	affinity	liking	dislike
4. represent	model	distort	exemplify
5. confusion	peacefulness	tranquility	serenity
6. fruitful	successful	abundant	failure
7. cautious	discreet	foolish	careful
8. mercenary	generous	selfish	greedy
9. careless	trustworthy	dependable	responsible
10. pleasant	amiable	mean	agreeable

2 Finish the story using the vocabulary words. Use each word once.

VOCABULARY LIST

exemplify	serenity	discreet	fruitful	mercenary
amiable	affinity	dependable	dour	submissive

I was a good baby-sitter. I had a(n) (1)_____ with children; I liked kids, and they liked me. I was also a(n) (2)_____ person. Parents could trust me to take care of their children. After a year of baby-sitting, I came to (3)_____ the kind of baby-sitter any parent would want. Then I met the triplets.

My (4)_____ was destroyed the minute their parents walked out the door. Matt jumped on the couch and started shouting, "I want chocolate—now, now, now!" I put him on the floor and told him he couldn't have chocolate before dinner. He kicked me. I was used to friendly and (5)_____ children. Matt's rude behavior shocked me. He ran off screaming, and I went looking for better luck with the other two kids. June was sitting on the kitchen floor with a(n) (6)_____ face. I bent down and said, "What's wrong, honey?" She pulled my hair, told me to mind my own business, and stomped off with the frown still glued on her face. I then saw Danny smiling at me. I knew that smile didn't mean he would be (7)_____ and do as I asked. It was obviously a malicious smile; he was just waiting to disobey me. I was defeated by five-year-olds. Or was I?

I looked in the freezer, refrigerator, and cupboards. I pulled out ice cream, cake, cookies, and chocolate bars and set them on the table. Matt and June appeared in seconds. All three kids began eating—and kept on eating. I made a(n) (8)_____ call home to check with my mom about my plan. She agreed that it was extreme, but sometimes extreme measures are needed. I returned to the kitchen and saw three kids holding their stomachs and moaning. My plan had been (9)_____ . The kids ate so much that they didn't argue with me one bit when I suggested they go to bed. I took them upstairs, tucked them in, and told them, "Sweet dreams." They groaned.

When their parents returned, I saw the surprised looks on their faces after I announced that the kids were in bed. I am not usually a(n) (10)_____ person, but I asked twice my usual fee, and they gladly paid. They asked me back for the next week, but I had decided to end my baby-sitting career on this last triumph.

3 Answer the following questions using the vocabulary words. Use each word once.

1. If you finish all your homework by noon, what has the morning been? _____

2. When directing a friend to remove a speck of food from her face, what is it usually polite to be? _____

3. If you agree to everything your friends want to do even if it isn't really what you want to do, what are you being? _____

4. If you enjoy spending your days at the beach or by a lake, what kind of relationship do you have with water? _____

5. If you are fun to be around, how might people describe you? _____

6. What kind of feeling might you experience while spending a weekend at a cabin in the woods? _____

7. After your favorite dog dies, how would you feel? _____

8. If you are never late and you never forget an appointment, what kind of person are you? _____

9. If you were hired as a member of a foreign country's army, what would your profession be? _____

10. If you were quiet at the theater in the hope that your younger brother and sister would be, too, what would you be trying to do? _____

Word Wise

A Different Approach

The Different Approach activities focus on various learning styles, so experiment with which activities work best for you. You can use these activities for a single chapter or to review several chapters.

Make Your Own Cloze

Equipment needed: paper and pen

Write your own cloze (a story with missing words) using six or seven of the words to be studied. Pick your own topic, or use one of the suggestions below. Try using some dialogue to make your story vivid. Exchange your story with a classmate; see if he or she can fill in the blanks. See if you can fill in the blanks of his or her story. When you are done, exchange papers again and check how many the person got right. Go over any wrong answers with each other to see what caused the mistake. Among the chapters you can refer to for examples of cloze tests are 2 (Self-Test 2) and 4 (Self-Test 3). For more on making your own tests, see the Hint in Chapter 5.

Suggested topics: The Destruction of a Planet, A Night of Mystery and Romance, A Favorite Book, A Trip Around the World, Traveling Back in Time

Interactive Exercise

Take a few minutes to complete the following questions on getting along with friends.

1. To achieve serenity with friends, what do you consider the most fruitful behavior for people to display?

   _____

   _____

2. What trait of a good friend does one of your friends exemplify? Give an example of a time your friend displayed this trait.

   _____

   _____

   _____

3. Do you feel that most people have an affinity with people who (Pick one.)

   _____ share all the same interests   _____ share some interests   _____ do not share any interests

4. What are two situations when friends shouldn't be submissive? How should they work out these problems or differences?

   _____

   _____

   _____

5. What qualities are important in a good friend? A good friend is (Mark all that apply.)

   _____ dependable   _____ apathetic   _____ dour   _____ patient

   _____ mercenary   _____ amiable   _____ discreet   _____ good-looking

---

HINT

Shades of Meaning

Learning new vocabulary is more than learning synonyms. While some words you learn may be similar to other words you know and may be used in place of another word, every word is unique. Good writers choose their words carefully. Words have different shades of meaning, and conscientious writers think about those differences when picking a word to use. A careful reader also responds to those differences in meaning. In some cases the differences are slight, such as "On Sundays I eat a big dinner" or "On Sundays I eat a large dinner." But replacing "big" or "large" with "huge" or "gigantic" (both synonyms for "big") does alter the image of how much food the person is eating. Some synonyms have even bigger differences. For the sentence, "The clever woman found a way to get out of debt," "clever" could be replaced with the synonyms "smart" or "crafty." The reader would have a different reaction to the woman depending on whether the writer selected "smart" or "crafty." When reading or writing, pay attention to the diverse ways words can be used.

Word List

affinity *n.* fondness; attachment; liking
[ə fin′ ə tē]

amiable *adj.* good-natured; agreeable
[ā′ mē ə bəl]

dependable *adj.* trustworthy; responsible
[di pen′ də bəl]

discreet *adj.* careful; cautious
[dis krēt′]

dour *adj.* dismal; gloomy; forbidding
[door, dour]

exemplify *v.* to show by example; to
[eg zem′ plə fī′, ig-] model; to represent

fruitful *adj.* successful; abundant
[froot′ fəl]

mercenary *adj.* selfish; greedy
[mûr′ sə ner′ ē] *n.* a professional soldier hired
to fight in a foreign army

serenity *n.* peacefulness, tranquility
[si ren′ ə tē]

submissive *adj.* obedient; passive
[səb mis′ iv]

Words to Watch

Which words would you like to practice with a bit more? Pick 3–5 words to study, and list them below. Write the word and its definition, and compose your own sentence using the word correctly. This extra practice could be the final touch to learning a word.

	Word	Definition	Your Sentence
1.	_____	_____	_____
	_____	_____	_____
2.	_____	_____	_____
	_____	_____	_____
3.	_____	_____	_____
	_____	_____	_____
4.	_____	_____	_____
	_____	_____	_____
5.	_____	_____	_____
	_____	_____	_____

Entertainment

Enjoying a Night Out

ENTERTAINMENT

Movie Sends Viewers to New Worlds

Planet Desire, rated PG-13, now playing at The Strand, Horizon, and Multiplex 11

Don't miss *Planet Desire*, a new action thriller. A
5   shy young man who spends his days alone in
front of his computer is drawn into a video game
thanks to a computer **glitch**. His sister discovers
the malfunction and sets out to save him despite
her **aversion** to technology. Breaking **protocol**,
10   she arranges a late-night **clandestine** meeting in
the woods with a computer genius who works for
a secret government agency. The genius finally
agrees to help by allowing her to play a **virtual**
reality game he has invented. He assures her that
15   the game is safe and that it will connect her to
her brother. Her only hope is to step into the
unknown, but can she trust this man? The plot
might sound wild, but it all feels real in the
theater. The acting, script, and special effects
20   make this a must-see movie, even if you aren't a
fan of technology.

**New Burger Place
Serves Up Fun**

Take a break from your **frenzied** studies and
head over to Pearl's for food and fun. Pearl's is a   25
great new burger place that is quickly becoming
popular with students. The menu features the
omnipresent hamburger, but Pearl's offers a few
unusual toppings. Some of the choices that may
intrigue you include blue cheese and gorgonzola   30
(cheddar and jack cheese are also available),
pineapple slices, jicama, and ice cream (yes, you
can have a dessert hamburger—it even comes
with a cherry on top). The menu also features
delicious fries, onion rings, Buffalo wings and a   35
variety of salads and sandwiches. Pearl's has ten
flavors of shakes. I give a standing **ovation** to
the banana shake: it's the best shake I've ever
tasted! Owner Pearl Barnes is a **resourceful**
woman. She has managed to fit twenty tables   40
and ten counter seats into the small space, but
the way she arranged everything the place doesn't
feel crowded, even on a busy Saturday night.
Come enjoy good food and fun people at Pearl's.

Located at 1543 Central Street, open for lunch   45
and dinner; low prices.

Predicting

For each set, write the definition on the line next to the word to which it belongs. If you are unsure, return to the reading on page 22, and underline any context clues you find. After you've made your predictions, check your answers against the Word List on page 27. Place a checkmark in the box next to each word whose definition you missed. These are the words you'll want to study closely.

Set One

simulated	a technical error	a strong dislike	private
a code of correct behavior			

- ☐ 1. **glitch** (line 7) _____
- ☐ 2. **aversion** (line 9) _____
- ☐ 3. **protocol** (line 9) _____
- ☐ 4. **clandestine** (line 10) _____
- ☐ 5. **virtual** (line 13) _____

Set Two

wild	present everywhere at once	approval	inventive	to fascinate

- ☐ 6. **frenzied** (line 24) _____
- ☐ 7. **omnipresent** (line 28) _____
- ☐ 8. **intrigue** (line 30) _____
- ☐ 9. **ovation** (line 37) _____
- ☐ 10. **resourceful** (line 39) _____

Self-Tests

1 Match each term with its synonym in Set One and its antonym in Set Two.

SYNONYMS

Set One

_____	1. glitch	a. private
_____	2. intrigue	b. malfunction
_____	3. omnipresent	c. etiquette
_____	4. clandestine	d. a plot
_____	5. protocol	e. everywhere

ANTONYM

Set Two

_____ 6. aversion   f. unimaginative

_____ 7. virtual   g. disapproval

_____ 8. resourceful   h. actual

_____ 9. frenzied   i. liking

_____ 10. ovation   j. calm

2 Complete the sentences using the vocabulary words. Use each word once.

VOCABULARY LIST

virtual	intrigue	clandestine	glitch	frenzied
ovation	omnipresent	aversion	resourceful	protocol

1. The crowd appreciated the outstanding perform-ance of the symphony, so they gave it a standing _____.

2. The drive was _____ as the couple tried to get to the airport on time after leaving late.

3. The spy held a(n) _____ meeting at midnight in an alley behind a warehouse.

4. There must be a(n) _____ in the computer; it never starts up correctly the first time.

5. Fran has a(n) _____ to talking to people because she is extremely shy.

6. Hamburger chains have become _____. You can see one on almost every corner in every town in America.

7. As a diplomat, Anthony learned the _____ for greeting a visiting king and queen.

8. Next semester I am taking a class from a(n) _____ college; it exists only online without any real buildings.

9. There was a lot of _____ at work last month as people tried to figure out who was going to become the new president of the company.

10. Milton is _____. I have seen him fix a car with chewing gum and a paper clip when we were stranded on the side of the road.

3 Fill in each blank with the letter of the most logical analogy. See Completing Analogies on page 6 for instructions and practice.

Set One

_____ 1. romance : clandestine ::

_____ 2. frenzied : peaceful ::

_____ 3. a technical problem : glitch ::

_____ 4. great musician : ovation ::

_____ 5. plot of a novel : intrigue ::

a. an excellent student : an "A"

b. sofa : couch

c. departing friend : sadden

d. sleepy : awake

e. a garden : overgrown

Set Two

_____ 6. diplomat : protocol ::

_____ 7. omnipresent : limited ::

_____ 8. computer games : virtual ::

_____ 9. aversion : snakes ::

_____ 10. resourceful : capable ::

f. fondness : cookies

g. beautiful : lovely

h. soldier : orders

i. jokes : funny

j. bitter : sweet

Word Wise

Collocations

Her car had become the *bane of* her *existence*. It was always breaking down when she most needed it. (Chapter 1)

The party will *be comprised of* a few of my closest friends from book club, school, and work. (Chapter 1) (Note: The structure *be comprised of* is considered informal by some people, and it may not be appropriate to use in all situations.)

Despite a *glitch in the system* at the beginning of the program that caused the stage to go black for ten minutes, the symphony still received a *standing ovation* at the end of the show. Every note had thrilled the crowd. (Chapter 3)

We may quite soon find *virtual reality* games in every home. We can play a game and really feel as if we are driving a racecar or diving underwater. (Chapter 3)

Interesting Etymologies

Bane (Chapter 1): comes from Old English *ban*, meaning "slayer, murderer," and from the Germanic *banjax*, meaning "wound." The tamer definition of "something that ruins or spoils" came into use in the late 1500s.

Interactive Exercise

Imagine that you are a movie or restaurant reviewer, and write a short review of a film you have recently seen or a restaurant where you like to eat. Use at least five of the vocabulary words in your review.

_____

_____

_____

_____

_____

_____

_____

_____

_____

_____

_____

_____

_____

Conversation Starters

An excellent way to review the vocabulary words and help to make them your own is to use them when you are speaking. Gather three to five friends or classmates, and use one or more of the conversation starters below. Before you begin talking, have each person write down six of the vocabulary words he or she will use during the conversation. Share your lists with each other to check that you did not all pick the same six words. Try to cover all of the words you want to study, whether you are reviewing one, two, or more chapters.

1. Which syllabus that you received this semester has been the most helpful? Why?

2. What troubles have you had with friends? What good times have you had with friends?

3. What movie or restaurant would you recommend to a friend? What makes it worth experiencing?

4. Tell about a memorable experience you have had this semester whether in the classroom, with friends, or while relaxing.

Word List

aversion
[ə vûr′ zhən, -shən]
n. 1. a strong dislike of something and a desire to avoid it; hatred
2. a cause or object of such a dislike

clandestine
[klan des′ tin]
adj. secret; private

frenzied
[fren′ zēd]
adj. wild; agitated; mad

glitch
[glich]
n. a minor malfunction or technical error

intrigue
[in′ trēg, in trēg′]
v. to fascinate
n. a scheme; a plot

omnipresent
[om′ ni prez′ ənt]
adj. present everywhere at once

ovation
[ō vā′ shən]
n. applause; approval

protocol
[prō′ tə kol′]
n. 1. a code of correct behavior; the etiquette diplomats follow
2. a plan for a medical treatment or scientific experiment
3. computer science: a standard method for controlling data transmission between computers

resourceful
[ri sôrs′ fəl]
adj. able to deal skillfully with new situations; capable; inventive

virtual
[vûr′ choo əl]
adj. 1. created or run by a computer; simulated
2. almost existing; near; practical
3. existing in the mind

Words to Watch

Which words would you like to practice with a bit more? Pick 3–5 words to study, and list them below. Write the word and its definition, and compose your own sentence using the word correctly. This extra practice could be the final touch to learning a word.

	Word	Definition	Your Sentence
1.			
2.			
3.			
4.			
5.			

Word Parts I

Look for words with these **prefixes**, **roots**, and/or **suffixes** as you work through this book. You may have already seen some of them, and you will see others in later chapters. Learning basic word parts can help you figure out the meanings of unfamiliar words.

prefix: a word part added to the beginning of a word that changes the meaning of the root

root: a word's basic part with its essential meaning

suffix: a word part added to the end of a word; indicates the part of speech

Word Part	Meaning	Examples and Definitions
Prefixes		
anti-	against	*antipathy:* dislike; a feeling against *antidote:* something that works against a disease
circum-	around, on all sides	*circumnavigate:* to go around *circumspect:* watchful; looking around
trans-	across	*transfer:* to carry across *transatlantic:* going across the Atlantic
Roots		
-cis-	to cut	*precise:* accurate; to the point; cut short *incisive:* cutting; penetrating
-claim-	to shout, to call out	*exclaim:* to shout; to speak suddenly *reclaim:* to call back; to rescue
-dur-	hard	*endure:* to tolerate hardship *durable:* lasting; hard
-fin-	end, limit	*finalist:* a person allowed to compete at the end of a contest *finite:* having an end or limit
Suffixes		
-ary (makes an adjective)	pertaining to or connected with	*mercenary:* pertaining to selfishness *sedentary:* connected with inactivity
-ify, -fy (makes a verb)	to make	*modify:* to make a change *clarify:* to make clear
-ity (makes a noun)	quality, state of being	*serenity:* quality of peacefulness *maternity:* the state of being a mother

1 Read each definition, and choose the appropriate word from the list below. Use each word once. The meaning of the word part is underlined to help you make the connection. Refer to the Word Parts list if you need help.

VOCABULARY LIST

ordinary	concise	obdurate	infinite	circumvent
antiwar	exclaim	transmit	magnify	celebrity

1. <u>against</u> combat _____

2. to <u>shout</u> _____

3. <u>pertaining to</u> the everyday _____

4. brief, <u>cut</u> short _____

5. <u>state of being</u> famous _____

6. to <u>make</u> bigger _____

7. unmoved, <u>hard</u> _____

8. to go <u>around</u> _____

9. <u>endless</u> _____

10. to send <u>across</u> _____

2 Finish the sentences with the meaning of each word part. Use each meaning once. The word part is underlined to help you make the connection.

VOCABULARY LIST

across	against	state of being	call out	connected with
cut	end	hard	make	around

1. If you <u>circum</u>navigate the globe, you sail _____ it.
2. An <u>auxi</u>liary group is _____ another group to give support.
3. If you <u>endure</u> a difficult class, you remain through the _____ times.
4. An <u>anti</u>-aging cream would work _____ getting older.
5. Scissors are used to _____ paper.
6. People often need to <u>transfer</u> from one bus to another when they take a trip _____ town.
7. When I <u>proclaim</u> to the class that I will study more often, I announce or _____ my plans.
8. If something is a <u>necess</u>ity, it has the _____ required.
9. If you <u>clarify</u> something, you _____ it easier to understand.
10. A <u>defin</u>itive answer would put a(n) _____ to a question.

3 Finish the story using the word parts. Use each word part once. Your knowledge of word parts, as well as the context clues, will help you create the correct words. If you do not understand the meaning of a word you have made, check your dictionary for the definition or to see whether the word exists.

WORD PARTS LIST				
circum	dur	ity	ary	cis
fin	ify	claim	anti	trans

AN ADVENTURE

I am usually a sedent(1)_____ person, but a friend of mine convinced me to take a combination hiking and camel-trekking trip with her. Due to various (2)_____stances, the time seemed right to try something new. It was near my thirtieth birthday, and I was beginning to see the (3)_____itory nature of life, so I figured "why not." I bought (4)_____able boots and a wide-brimmed hat, and I was ready to go.

I thought I might have to ver(5)_____ my sanity when I first saw the line of camels approaching. I was going to ride one of those? The first day, however, was great. The guide said I was riding like I had been doing it since I was born. I was getting a little too confident, and my humil(6)_____ returned on day three. I fell off my camel with a big thud. I skinned my left knee and elbow. Luckily, I wasn't hurt worse. The guide cleaned me up and put some (7)_____septic on my wounds. I was good to go again. I tried to re(8)_____ some of my dignity by making it safely to the next campsite.

I wasn't feeling too sure about continuing the next day, but our guide had an idea. He made two small in(9)_____ions in my saddle and wrapped a piece of rope through them to make a seatbelt for me. He said I could use it until I got my confidence back. By the afternoon I didn't need it, and the rest of the trip was wonderful. I'm de(10)_____itely going to spend the rest of my life having more adventures and seeing new places.

4 Pick the best definition for each underlined word using your knowledge of word parts. Circle the word part in each of the underlined words.

a. cutting; penetrating

b. to make invalid

c. limit

d. crossing the sea

e. distance around

f. against being with others

g. quality of being dishonest

h. hardship; pressure

i. pertaining to the power to judge

j. denied a connection

_____ 1. The judge threw out the case after he learned that the man had confessed under <u>duress</u>.

_____ 2. The <u>circumference</u> of the circle was hard to figure out because I forgot the formula.

_____ 3. The lawyer's questions were so <u>incisive</u> that the defendant was unable to hide what happened at the murder scene.

_____ 4. The <u>transoceanic</u> voyage took us a week. It was a peaceful vacation.

_____ 5. After the roof fell in on the cabin, my brother <u>disclaimed</u> owning any part of it.

_____ 6. My teacher said to <u>confine</u> my research paper to one story I had read this semester.

_____ 7. My mother says I am <u>antisocial</u>, but I prefer to stay home and read instead of go to parties.

_____ 8. After my mother died, my father decided to <u>nullify</u> his will and make a brand new one.

_____ 9. I discovered my friend's <u>duplicity</u> when I saw him kissing my girlfriend.

_____ 10. My dad made an <u>arbitrary</u> decision that I should be home from my date by nine o'clock.

5 A good way to remember word parts is to pick one word that uses a word part and understand how that word part functions in the word. Then you can apply that meaning to other words that have the same word part. Use the following words to help you match the word part to its meaning.

SET ONE

_____ 1. **anti-**: antipathy, antiseptic, antidote

_____ 2. **-claim-**: exclaim, proclaim, reclaim

_____ 3. **circum-**: circumnavigate, circumvent, circumstances

_____ 4. **-dur-**: endure, durable, obdurate

_____ 5. **-ary**: mercenary, arbitrary, emissary

a. hard

b. to shout, to call out

c. against

d. around, on all sides

e. pertaining to or connected with

SET TWO

_____ 6. **-fin-**: finalist, definitive, confine

_____ 7. **trans-**: transfer, translate, transmit

_____ 8. **-cis-**: incisive, concise, scissors

_____ 9. **-ity**: serenity, duplicity, celebrity

_____ 10. **-ify, -fy**: modify, magnify, exemplify

f. to make

g. to cut

h. end, limit

i. across

j. quality, state of being

Interactive Exercise ||||||||||||||||||||||||||||||||||||||||||||||||||||||||||||||||

Use the dictionary to find a word you don't know that uses each word part listed below. Write the meaning of the word part, the word, and the definition. If your dictionary has the etymology (history) of the word, see how the word part relates to the meaning, and write the etymology after the definition.

Word Part	Meaning	Word	Definition and Etymology
EXAMPLE:			
-fin-	end, limit	finial	a small ending ornament at the top of a gable, arch, spire, or other object; from the Latin "finis," meaning "end"
1. anti-			
2. circum-			
3. trans-			
4. -fin-			
5. -dur-			

Word Wise

Internet Activity: Creating a Blog

You can use the Internet to develop your vocabulary by writing e-mails to classmates or friends that contain the vocabulary words or get several class members to agree on a time to be on the Internet and instant message each other to feel like you are using the words in a conversation. You can also explore the world of Web logs, or blogs for short.

In the last few years, blogs have become increasingly popular. A blog is an online journal. It is a Web site where you can express your thoughts on whatever interests you: sports, politics, music. Other people on the Web can read your blog, make comments back to you, and link your site to theirs. A blog gives you a chance to express your opinions, share your creative writing, or find others with similar interests. You can also add photographs and create links to Web sites you enjoy.

Starting a blog is easy. Try blogger.com or LiveJournal.com to get started; both are free services. You can even create a group blog, so you can get several classmates or the whole class involved. Just go through the steps listed on the site, and you can be blogging in five minutes. Make a conscious effort to use the week's vocabulary words in your blog. To make comments to each other, again using the vocabulary words, get the addresses of at least two other students' blogs.

Remember to be careful about the personal information you share on the Web. You can create a profile of yourself on your blog. Avoid giving out information such as your address and phone number and, of course, passwords. You may want to create a new e-mail address to use when you set up your blog. See Chapter 13 for information on Internet scams. Enjoy the ability to communicate with a wide audience, but be alert for those who want to abuse the power of the Internet.

HINT

Etymologies

An etymology is the history of a word. Some dictionaries at the end of an entry will tell how the word came into existence. There are several ways words are developed, such as being made up, coming from a person's name, or evolving over time from foreign languages. Reading a word's etymology can sometimes help you remember the meaning. For example, the word **addict** comes from the Latin *addictus*, which meant someone given to another as a slave. This history helps to show how being addicted to something is being a slave to it. Not all words have interesting histories, but taking the time to read an etymology can be useful. If you get excited about word origins, there are books available on the subject that show how fascinating words can be.

5

Review

Focus on Chapters 1–4

The following activities give you a chance to interact some more with the vocabulary words you've learned. By looking at art, taking tests, answering questions, doing a crossword puzzle, and working with others, you will see which words you know well and which you still need to work with.

Art

Match each picture below to one of the following vocabulary words. Use each word once.

VOCABULARY LIST

syllabus	dour	ovation
aversion	berate	serenity

1. _____

2. _____

3. _____

4. _____

5. _____

6. _____

Self-Tests

1 Pick the word that best completes each sentence.

1. I wasn't sure of company _____, so I called my manager to find out if I could take a client to lunch.

   a. ovation   b. serenity   c. protocol   d. syllabus

2. I don't consider myself a(n) _____ person, but I don't like to pay more than my fair share when we split the bill at lunch.

   a. mercenary   b. virtual   c. amiable   d. zealous

3. I need to stop _____ myself when I do poorly on a test and start studying more.

   a. intriguing   b. exemplifying   c. indicating   d. berating

4. Early mornings are the _____ of my work life. Why can't meetings be held in the afternoon?

   a. apathy   b. mercenary   c. glitch   d. bane

5. When I noticed people whispering in the halls, I knew there was some _____ going on at work.

   a. intrigue   b. serenity   c. glitch   d. terminology

2 Pick the vocabulary word that best completes the sentence. Use each word once.

a. zealous	b. amiable	c. virtual	d. dour	e. omnipresent

1. Margaret is usually a pleasant person, but she wasn't that _____ at the party last night. I wonder if something is wrong with her.

2. I decided to avoid Roger at work until his _____ expression disappeared.

3. The food seemed to be _____ at the party, or maybe it just felt that way because I was on a diet.

4. The woman was _____ about running; she went out even when two feet of snow covered the ground.

5. The _____ program shows that our company could be more efficient if we rearrange our work spaces.

3 Finish the story using the vocabulary words below. Use each word once.

VOCABULARY LIST

affinity	apathy	aversion	dependable	durable
exemplified	frenzied	resourceful	submissive	undermine

APPRECIATING NATURE

I used to have a(n) (1)_____ to sleeping on the ground. And at best I had (2)_____ toward carrying a pack on my back, but when I dropped off friends for an overnight hike at Hidden Glen, I was intrigued by the beauty at the start of the hike. My friend said the lovely wooded pathway (3)_____ the rest of the area. He told me about forests to explore, meadows to wander in, and streams to camp near. He also said I was too much of a wimp to ever join them. I decided then that I wouldn't let his comments (4)_____ my desire to see what was beyond the path.

I went out the next day and bought a strong and (5)_____ backpack. The clerk said that it would give me years of enjoyment. He also helped me pick out some other equipment that he said every (6)_____ hiker should have. Two weeks later, after a(n) (7)_____ night of packing and repacking, I was ready the next morning when my friends picked me up. On that first hike I was pretty (8)_____ and did whatever my friends told me. Now, after five years of backpacking, I have become a (n) (9)_____ leader, and I make a lot of the decisions. I have also discovered that I have a real (10)_____ for nature.

Interactive Exercise |||||||||||||||||||||||||||||||||||||||||||||||||||||||||||||||||||

Answer the following questions to further test your understanding of the vocabulary words.

1. What are two signs that would indicate a person is interested in meeting you? _____

   _____

2. What are two essential materials needed for a fruitful study session? _____

   _____

3. Where would you hold a clandestine meeting in your town? Why is it a good place for such a

   meeting? _____

   _____

4. Name two courses where you have had to learn new terminology. _____

   _____

5. What is something people should be discreet about? _____

   _____

6. What would you do if there was a glitch in your computer system the night before you had a

   paper due? _____

   _____

7. What activities would your perfect day comprise? _____

   _____

8. What do you do to restore your serenity after a busy week? _____

   _____

9. How often do you refer to a syllabus for a class? Do you use one syllabus more than others?

   _____

10. What does a performer need to do to get a standing ovation from you? _____

    _____

HINT

Make Your Own Tests

A great way to study is to make your own tests in the same style of the tests that you will have in class. Making the tests puts you in the instructor's frame of mind and makes you think about what is important to study.

- Before the first test (or quiz), ask your instructor what format(s) the test will be in—true/false, multiple choice, matching, essay.
- Create a test in the same format(s) with questions that you think will be asked, neatly hand-written or typed. Set the test aside for a day.
- The next day, take the test and correct yourself. How much did you remember?
- Make a test for a friend, and exchange tests with each other. Did you come up with similar questions?
- If you examine the first in-class test, you will have a better idea of what the instructor is look-ing for, and then your homemade tests will be even more useful.

Crossword Puzzle

Use the following words to complete the crossword puzzle. Use each word once.

VOCABULARY LIST

affinity	indicate
amiable	intrigue
bane	omnipresent
clandestine	submissive
comprise	undermine
discreet	virtual
exemplify	zealous
glitch	

Across

1. almost existing
6. to weaken by small stages
7. careful
10. to represent
13. to show the need for
15. a meeting in a dark alley

Down

2. fondness
3. present everywhere at once
4. agreeable
5. to be composed of
8. I'll do whatever you say.
9. a minor technical error
11. a deadly poison
12. I'm eager to go!
14. James Bond is always involved in

Mix It Up

Matching Meanings

Get four to six classmates together, and make teams of two to three people. You will need two sets of flash cards. Lay out a square of 25 flash cards with the words face up. Lay out another square of the same 25 words with the definitions face up. (You can make larger or smaller squares, but it is best to have at least fifteen words, and no more than forty.) One person on a team picks up a word and tries to find the matching definition in the other square. Teammates can help the person. If the person is right, he or she gets to keep both cards. If the person is wrong, he or she returns the cards to their places. A team can keep going until it misses a match. When all the words and definitions are matched, the team with the most cards wins. This activity can also be played with pairs, or you can test yourself individually if you have two sets of flash cards (or you can write the words on slips of paper and match them to the definition side of your flash cards).

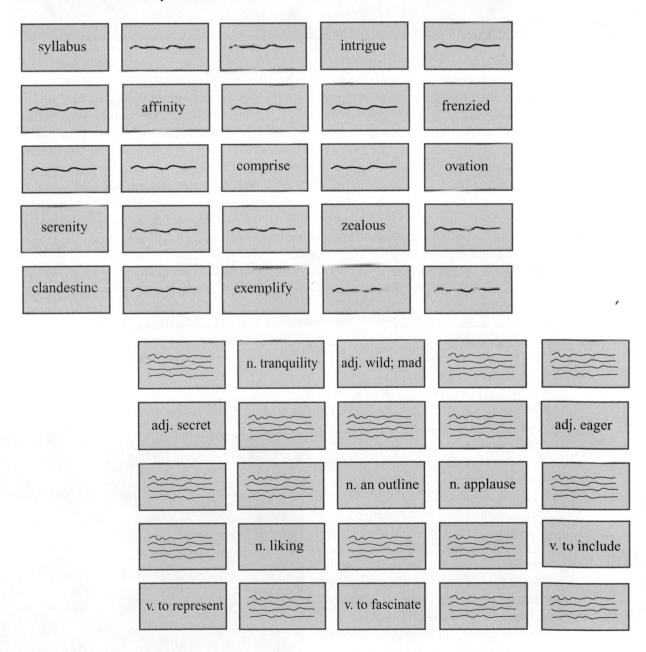

6

Science Fiction

The Silent Stars

They had lost contact with the Earth. The crew didn't know this yet, but they would soon. They had been sent to **subjugate** the newly discovered life on Jupiter. Conquering another race was not a mission that Orion enjoyed. He never believed that humans were the **omnipotent** race, but the government felt otherwise, and it was impossible to resist its force. He was told that if he wanted to voice
5 any **dissent**, he would find himself in prison. Rather than disagree, he took the assignment.

His lack of enthusiasm for the job had led to a **cursory** inspection of the ship's equipment. Now he regretted the rush, although no longer being under the Earth's surveillance might have its benefits. Orion checked with his chief engineer to see whether the **precise** reason for the malfunction could be discovered. It wasn't a problem with the communication equipment after all; it was a **miscalculation**
10 by the navigation computer that had sent the ship off course. No one knew where they were, and they were no longer within range to communicate with any satellites.

He could already feel the Grand Commander's anger. When, or if, they returned, he was sure the commander would **annihilate** the whole crew. The commander's **antipathy** for those who failed was well known. He had all too often destroyed whole fleets for failing a mission. It was time for Orion to
15 make a decision.

Just as he was to announce to the crew that there was a glitch in the navigation system and that their mission was about to change, Sergeant Aurora escorted Private Gemini into the room.

"Sir, we discovered what caused the problem with the navigation computer. Private Gemini introduced a virus into the program."
20 Amazed, all Orion could ask was "Why?"

With absolute serenity, Private Gemini explained, "I can't go on another mission to take over an innocent planet. We haven't the right."

"Your motive may be honorable Private, but I can't **condone** such behavior. I will have
25 to put you in confinement. Take her away."

When he was alone, Orion smiled. He would release the clever and attractive private in a couple days. He would soon interview her more thoroughly to see what she
30 had done to the computer, but in his heart he felt she had helped them all. They were now **emissaries** for peace. It was time to finally tell the crew that they were headed on a mission of discovery and that they would be
35 bringing a message of peace to those they encountered among the stars.

Predicting

For each set, write the definition on the line next to the word to which it belongs. If you are unsure, return to the reading on page 40, and underline any context clues you find. After you've made your predictions, check your answers against the Word List on page 45. Place a checkmark in the box next to each word whose definition you missed. These are the words you'll want to study closely.

Set One

having unlimited authority or power	exact	to differ in opinion	to conquer	hasty

☐ 1. **subjugate** (line 2) _____

☐ 2. **omnipotent** (line 3) _____

☐ 3. **dissent** (line 5) _____

☐ 4. **cursory** (line 6) _____

☐ 5. **precise** (line 8) _____

Set Two

to destroy	to forgive	a mistake in planning	dislike	representatives sent on a mission

☐ 6. **miscalculation** (line 9) _____

☐ 7. **annihilate** (line 13) _____

☐ 8. **antipathy** (line 13) _____

☐ 9. **condone** (line 24) _____

☐ 10. **emissaries** (line 32) _____

Self-Tests

1 Circle the correct word to complete each sentence.

1. The dictator tried to (annihilate, subjugate) the people so they would work in the fields.

2. I realized I needed to do more than a (precise, cursory) proofreading of my papers after I got a "D" on my first essay.

3. Because of one little (antipathy, miscalculation), we ended up twenty miles from where we wanted to be.

4. I can't (dissent, condone) the newspaper's sloppy coverage of the city's plans for downtown redevelopment; it has not investigated how the changes are going to affect those who live downtown.

5. I didn't like it when Debbie was my baby-sitter because she thought she was (cursory, omnipotent).

6. I wanted to (annihilate, condone) the crab grass; it was ruining an otherwise beautiful lawn.

7. I have an (antipathy, emissary) for spicy mustards on my sandwiches.

8. Since the two countries were at war, the (miscalculation, emissary) secretly met with the king to discuss plans to settle the dispute.

9. I am (precise, omnipotent) when I make a catalogue order so I don't get the wrong items.

10. I had to (subjugate, dissent) when asked if I agreed with moving the meeting to Thursday; I already had plans for that day.

2 Match the quotation to the word it best illustrates. Context clues are underlined to help you. Use each word once.

Set One

VOCABULARY LIST

| annihilate | antipathy | emissary | condone | miscalculation |

1. "I hate shopping. How can some people spend all day at a mall?" _____

2. "I will deliver your message to the president when I meet with her next week after my return home." _____

3. "I thought if we left at three o'clock we would have plenty of time to make it by five. I forgot about the bridge construction delay. I planned wrong, again." _____

4. "I can overlook your coming home late this time since you helped your sick friend get home safely." _____

5. "We destroyed that team 63 to 0." _____

Set Two

VOCABULARY LIST

| omnipotent | dissent | cursory | precise | subjugate |

6. "You must be accurate when you take these pills: take the red pill at noon every day and the blue pill at 10 a.m. every other day." _____

7. "I have conquered your country—bow down before me!" _____

8. "I looked the report over quickly, Doris, and it seems fine." _____

9. "I beg to differ with the committee. I think the plan will work." _____

10. "As fire chief, the City Council has given me full authority to handle the spreading wild fires." _____

3 Use the vocabulary words to complete the following analogies. See Completing Analogies on page 6 for instructions and practice.

Set One

VOCABULARY LIST

| cursory | dissent | annihilate | antipathy | emissary |

1. grow : flowers :: _____ : weeds

2. friend : warmth :: enemy : _____

3. accept : reject :: _____ : accurate

4. mother : scolding :: _____ : message

5. assent : agree :: _____ : differ

VOCABULARY LIST

subjugate	condone	miscalculation	precise	omnipotent

6. baker : cake :: tired person : _____
7. distant : close :: _____ : powerless
8. fortunate : lucky :: exact : _____
9. crown : a king :: _____ : a slave
10. rain : flowers :: special circumstances : _____

Word Wise

Context Clue Mini-Lesson 2

This lesson uses antonyms—words that mean the opposite of the unknown word—as the clues. In the paragraph below, circle the antonyms you find for the underlined words and then, on the lines that follow the paragraph, write a word that is opposite the antonym as your definition of the word.

The opening night of the new art exhibit didn't start well. I saw a man grimace as he studied a painting of bright yellow and orange flowers. What was wrong? Most people would smile at such a scene. I heard a woman swear behind me. I wondered what painting could have incensed her so; most of the works were meant to calm people. I was feeling despondent. Looking for a way to cheer myself up, I spied the refreshment table. The pastries I had ordered from the new bakery looked delicious. I took a bite and finally understood what was upsetting people. Instead of sugar, the bakery had put salt in the icing. I would not, however, let my guests forsake me because of a salty pastry. I threw the tray in the trash and sent my assistant to buy cookies. I persuaded those in attendance to remain with promises of special deals and more goodies to come.

Your Definition

1. Grimace _____
2. Incensed _____
3. Despondent _____
4. Forsake _____

Write your own science fiction story. Use at least seven of the vocabulary words in your story. Subjects to consider include meeting aliens, interacting with robots, exploring planets, and traveling through time.

_____

_____

_____

_____

_____

_____

_____

_____

_____

_____

_____

Word Part Reminder

Below are a few short exercises to help you review the word parts you have been learning. Fill in the missing word part from the list, and circle the meaning of the word part found in each sentence. Try to complete the questions without returning to the Word Parts chapter, but if you get stuck, look back at Chapter 4.

Example: I am (against) sweating much, so I use an _anti_perspirant each morning.

       trans   cis   dur   fy

1. I wanted to make my stomach happy, and the only thing I felt that would satis_____ it was a slice of pizza.

2. Even though we lived across town from each other, my partner and I were easily able to _____act business with the aid of phones, computers, and fax machines.

3. Before he began to cut material for a suit, my uncle would check his measurements three times. Because he was so pre_____e, he never made a mistake.

4. It is hard to persuade my grandfather to try a new restaurant. He is so ob_____ate that he doesn't like to do anything unless he is the one who suggests it.

Word List

annihilate
[ə nī′ ə lāt′]
v. to destroy; to defeat completely

antipathy
[an tip′ ə thē]
n. an aversion; an opposition in feeling; dislike

condone
[kən dōn′]
v. 1. to forgive or pardon; to excuse
2. to overlook; to ignore something illegal or offensive; to give unstated approval to

cursory
[kûr′ sə rē]
adj. going rapidly over something, without noticing details; hasty; superficial

dissent
[di sent′]
v. to differ in feeling or opinion, especially from the majority
n. a difference of opinion

emissary
[em′ ə ser′ ē]
n. 1. a representative sent on a mission; a delegate
2. an agent sent on a secret mission

miscalculation
[mis kal′ kyə lā′ shən]
n. a mistake in planning or forecasting

omnipotent
[om nip′ ə tənt]
adj. having great or unlimited authority or power

precise
[pri sīs′]
adj. 1. exact; accurate; definite
2. strictly correct; demanding

subjugate
[sub′ jə gāt′]
v. to conquer; to master; to dominate

Words to Watch

Which words would you like to practice with a bit more? Pick 3–5 words to study, and list them below. Write the word and its definition, and compose your own sentence using the word correctly. This extra practice could be the final touch to learning a word.

Word	Definition	Your Sentence
1.		
2.		
3.		
4.		
5.		

Romance

A Knock on the Door

Estella slowly opens the door. It is one o'clock in the morning—who could possibly be knocking so forcefully? Little does she know the **pandemonium** that is going to
5 disturb her quiet night. Her big brown eyes open wide when she sees Byron's **virile** build fill the doorway. His manliness causes Estella's heart to pound as loudly as his knocking on the door. It has been four
10 months since they broke up, but she is once again in an **amorous** mood after admiring Byron's strong frame.

"I must see you," he gasps.

The **provocative** look in his eyes is one
15 Estella cannot resist. She motions him inside and shuts the door.

Byron stumbles to the couch and collapses. Estella sees the blood stain on Byron's chest. She tears off her robe and
20 presses it against his rippling muscles, so easily apparent under the damp shirt. Due to Estella's quick actions, Byron revives.

"Estella, I need your help. If you no longer **abhor** me, please, please, hide me."

25 "Oh, Byron, I don't hate you. You know you have come to the perfect place for **seclusion**. Let's not **delude** ourselves any longer. We are a good team, and we were fooling ourselves by thinking we could work or love better alone."

30 "I love you, too, Estella. Unfortunately, there is no time to **embellish** my story, even though it is a good one. The simple truth is I am being chased by . . ."

Estella smiles and pulls Byron to her. **Oblivious** to the danger close by, they embrace. A pounding at the door soon shatters their **euphoria**.

"We know you're in there, Byron. We're breaking down the door."

Predicting

For each set, write the definition on the line next to the word to which it belongs. If you are unsure, return to the reading on page 46, and underline any context clues you find. After you've made your predictions, check your answers against the Word List on page 51. Place a checkmark in the box next to each word whose definition you missed. These are the words you'll want to study closely.

Set One

to hate	passionate	strong	chaos	exciting

- ☐ 1. **pandemonium** (line 4) _____
- ☐ 2. **virile** (line 6) _____
- ☐ 3. **amorous** (line 11) _____
- ☐ 4. **provocative** (line 14) _____
- ☐ 5. **abhor** (line 24) _____

Set Two

to add details	to fool	a feeling of extreme happiness	unaware	a sheltered place

- ☐ 6. **seclusion** (line 27) _____
- ☐ 7. **delude** (line 27) _____
- ☐ 8. **embellish** (line 30) _____
- ☐ 9. **oblivious** (line 32) _____
- ☐ 10. **euphoria** (line 33) _____

Self-Tests

1 In each group, there are three synonyms and one antonym. Circle the antonym.

1. unaware	oblivious	attentive	forgetful
2. provocative	boring	exciting	stimulating
3. manly	weak	strong	virile
4. adore	hate	abhor	detest
5. delude	trick	mislead	trust
6. joy	euphoria	sadness	jubilation
7. chaos	disorder	peace	pandemonium

8.	isolation	exposure	solitude	seclusion
9.	cold	amorous	loving	passionate
10.	elaborate	exaggerate	embellish	minimize

2 Finish these tabloid headlines using the vocabulary words. Use each word once.

VOCABULARY LIST

| virile | oblivious | embellish | provocative | amorous |
| delude | pandemonium | seclusion | abhors | euphoria |

1. _____ *Couple Caught in Embarrassing Position on Parade Float*

2. Two-Headed Beast of the Northwest Seeks _____ from Curious Tourists

3. Elvis Discovered Working in the Produce Section: _____ Breaks Out in Memphis Grocery

4. _____ Young Man Lifts House Off Child

5. Gone for Six Months: Wife _____ to Missing Husband

6. *New _____ Red Leather Police Uniforms Banned in Four States*

7. _____ on the Farm with Birth of First Self-Milking Cow

8. *Dixie Lee Jean Predicts Billionaire Husband Will _____ Wife about Real Purpose of Business Trips*

9. Latin Teen Idol Announces He _____ Samba Music

10. Forty Varieties of Flowers, a Dozen Peacocks, One Thousand Pink Balloons _____ Film Star's Wedding

3 Write the vocabulary word on the line next to the situation it best illustrates. Use each word once. Imagine each scene begins with "When a person..."

Set One

VOCABULARY LIST

amorous	abhor	euphoria	delude	oblivious

1. wins the lottery _____
2. has to stand in a long line _____
3. crosses the street in front of a car _____
4. thinks he or she can write a great research paper in an hour _____
5. feels like French kissing _____

Set Two

VOCABULARY LIST

embellish	seclusion	pandemonium	virile	provocative

6. wants to spend the summer in a cabin in the woods _____
7. starts bullfighting _____
8. says that the walk to the corner store was fifty miles, all uphill, through fields of cactus, in the burning sun _____
9. asks whether all drugs should be legal _____
10. is faced with a room full of five-year-olds at a birthday party

Word Wise

Internet Activity: How Often Is It Used?

Here is an activity that will illustrate different contexts for the vocabulary words and emphasize the enormity of the Internet. Type a vocabulary word into a search engine such as Google or Yahoo. See how many times the word is found. Read through the first few entries and see how the word is used. Find a Web site that seems interesting. Open it and look for the word again to see it in its full context. For example, the word *amiable* turned up 5,410,000 results. Among the first few entries, it was used in the contexts of a clothing line, a limousine service, dog training classes, and on a site that describes customer personality types. Sometimes you will get a lot more results. *Phishing* turned up 18,600,000 results. And sometimes the results can be surprising. For *lax* several of the 27,900,000 results had to deal with LAX (Los Angeles International Airport) and quite a few with lacrosse. Have fun seeing what is out there.

Your word: _____

Number of results: _____

A sample context: _____

Name of the Web site you visited: _____

Share your finds with classmates. What words did people pick to look up? Which had the least results, and which had the most? Did anyone find a really interesting site?

Interactive Exercise

Put yourself into the author's chair by answering the following questions.

1. What kind of pandemonium breaks out when the door is opened?

   _____

2. If Byron had time to embellish his story, who would he say is chasing him?

   _____

3. What virile activities will they need to engage in to escape?

   _____

4. Has Byron deluded Estella about anything?

   _____

5. What kinds of danger will the couple have to be oblivious to in order to succeed?

   _____

6. What provocative question will Byron ask Estella at some point in their adventure?

   _____

7. Where do they go to find seclusion?

   _____

8. Will Byron and Estella have any amorous meetings during their escape?

   _____

9. Will they abhor or love each other when their adventure is over? Why?

   _____

   _____

10. Will they find euphoria or tragedy at the end of the story? Explain.

   _____

   _____

HINT

More Choices

If want to read more for pleasure, here are some excellent writers of science fiction, romance, and mysteries to get you started:

Science Fiction

Isaac Asimov	The Foundation Trilogy; I, Robot
Ray Bradbury	Fahrenheit 451; The Martian Chronicles
Ursula K. Le Guin	The Left Hand of Darkness; The Dispossessed

Romance

Jane Austen	Pride and Prejudice; Emma
Laura Esquivel	Like Water for Chocolate; Swift As Desire: A Novel
Thomas Hardy	Return of the Native; Tess of the D'Urbervilles

Mysteries

Agatha Christie	Murder on the Orient Express; And Then There Were None
Tony Hillerman	A Thief of Time; The Dance Hall of the Dead
Walter Mosley	Devil in a Blue Dress; A Little Yellow Dog

Word List

abhor
[ab hôr′]

v. to detest; to loathe; to hate

amorous
[am′ ər əs]

adj. being in love; passionate

delude
[di lōōd′]

v. to mislead; to deceive; to fool

embellish
[em bel′ ish, im-]

v. 1. to exaggerate; to elaborate; to add details
2. to decorate

euphoria
[yōō fôr′ ē ə, -fōr′ ē ə]

n. a feeling of extreme well-being or extreme happiness

oblivious
[ə bliv′ ē əs]

adj. unaware; forgetful

pandemonium
[pan′ də mō′ nē əm]

n. disorder; chaos

provocative
[prə vok′ ə tiv]

adj. stimulating; exciting; troubling

seclusion
[si klōō′ zhən]

n. solitude; a sheltered place

virile
[vir′ əl]

adj. masculine; manly; strong

Words to Watch

Which words would you like to practice with a bit more? Pick 3–5 words to study, and list them below. Write the word and its definition, and compose your own sentence using the word correctly. This extra practice could be the final touch to learning a word.

	Word	Definition	Your Sentence
1.			
2.			
3.			
4.			
5.			

Mystery

Missing from the Mound

I had **misgivings** about accepting this case from the beginning. I'm not much of a sports fan, so I wasn't sure I was the
5　right detective to go looking for a missing pitcher. But an old friend of mine was working PR for the team, and she knew I would keep the case a secret.
10　The team didn't want anyone to find out its star pitcher was missing three days before the playoffs began. I promised Tess that I would keep my investiga-
15　tion **covert**. It was going to make it more difficult to question people, but I'd manage.

My first call was to the pitcher's wife. She quickly **assented** to an interview in a bar near the stadium. I had a **presentiment** that the interview wasn't going to go smoothly. By the time I arrived, she
20　looked to be drowning her sorrows in her fifth or sixth martini. I asked about her husband's activities the day he went missing. She started rambling about their marital problems and how he wasn't any good to her. When she got to the point, I found out that they'd had a huge fight that morning about an affair he'd been having with the team owner's daughter. He stormed out of the house, and she hadn't seen him since.

25　I decided to **circumvent** the usual routes to meeting Lola McCurvy, the owner's daughter, by staking out her favoring beauty salon. I don't like to deal with a lot of personal assistants and such when I need to talk to someone. Miss McCurvy seemed quite **incredulous** that I would want to speak with her about Thompson.

"Why talk to me? My relationship with George was a **transitory** affair. It only lasted for a couple
30　of months. I dumped him over three weeks ago," she purred.

"What were you doing Monday between 10 am and 8 pm?" I asked.

"If you are asking if I have an **alibi**, I'm afraid it isn't a great one. I wasn't feeling well that day, so I stayed home in bed. My maid came in a couple of times to bring me a cup of tea and a snack. You can check with her."

35　"Oh, I will."

I'm usually an **optimist**, which is rare for a PI, but I was beginning to doubt whether I'd find Thompson before the playoffs began, and if I did, whether he'd be alive. I was going to have to take **decisive** steps to track him down. I needed to interview his teammates one by one starting with the first baseman Hernandez. It was widely known that he and Thompson had a strong aversion to each
40　other. It was going to be a long day.

Predicting

For each set, write the definition on the line next to the word to which it belongs. If you are unsure, return to the reading on page 52, and underline any context clues you find. After you've made your predictions, check your answers against the Word List on page 57. Place a checkmark in the box next to each word whose definition you missed. These are the words you'll want to study closely.

Set One

| agreed | feelings of doubt | to go around | secret | a feeling that something is about to happen |

☐ 1. **misgivings** (line 1) _____

☐ 2. **covert** (line 15) _____

☐ 3. **assented** (line 18) _____

☐ 4. **presentiment** (line 19) _____

☐ 5. **circumvent** (line 25) _____

Set Two

| a person who looks on the bright side | definite | temporary | disbelieving | an excuse or explanation |

☐ 6. **incredulous** (line 27) _____

☐ 7. **transitory** (line 29) _____

☐ 8. **alibi** (line 32) _____

☐ 9. **optimist** (line 36) _____

☐ 10. **decisive** (line 38) _____

Self-Tests

1 Circle the correct word to complete each sentence.

1. The woman was certainly (decisisve, incredulous). She decided on the color to paint her bathroom after looking at three samples for two minutes.

2. The operation was (transitory, covert), so Gerry couldn't tell any of his friends about his mission.

3. As the leaves fall off the trees, I am reminded of the (decisive, transitory) beauty of autumn.

4. It is good to be (incredulous, covert) when someone says you can easily get rich.

5. I had a great (presentiment, alibi): I was speaking in front of two hundred people when the robbery took place.

6. Most people would (assent, optimist) to being given a million dollars.

7. Thelma tried to avoid taking a placement test; she wanted to (covert, circumvent) the college's procedures.

8. After Darlene found out her fiance had cheated on her, she had (misgivings, assent) about marrying him.

9. Vicky was nevous about getting in the car. She had a (presentiment, circumvent) that she would be in an accident.

10. Eddy is the eternal (alibi, optimist). Even when it is pouring rain, he is sure that it will clear up in time for a picnic.

2 Detectives often have questions or other thoughts running through their minds when they're trying to solve a crime. Write the vocabulary word that connects to the following thoughts the private investigator has about the case. Context clues are underlined to help you. Use each word once.

VOCABULARY LIST

alibi	presentiment	circumvent	covert	decisive
assent	incredulous	misgiving	optimist	transitory

1. I'm glad the witness <u>agreed</u> to be interviewed. _____
2. I'm <u>skeptical</u> that Thompson's wife told me the whole story about their fight. _____
3. The team manager <u>was in meetings Monday from 8 a.m. until 10 p.m.</u> _____
4. I need to find a way <u>to avoid</u> the security guard so I can look around the locker room undisturbed. _____
5. I really <u>feel like I will find Thompson tomorrow.</u> _____
6. Did Thompson disappear because he had <u>a feeling that something bad was about to happen?</u> _____
7. I may have to <u>conceal</u> myself somewhere in the clubhouse to discover any team secrets. _____
8. The team owner's answers weren't very <u>definite.</u> Was he trying to cover something up, or does he just not know much about the team? _____
9. I need to search Thompson's locker right away because things <u>may change quickly</u> if anyone discovers he is missing. _____
10. Why do I have <u>a feeling of distrust</u> about Miss McCurvy's story that her maid brought her tea? _____

3 Finish the story using the vocabulary words. Use each word once.

VOCABULARY LIST

alibi	transitory	assented	misgivings	optimist
circumvent	covert	decisive	incredulous	presentiment

I had a(n) (1) _____ that something bad was going to happen while we were on vacation. My wife thought my (2) _____ were silly, but after I kept on about them for three days, she (3) _____ to going home early. When we got home, we were shocked that all our living room furniture was missing. At first my wife was (4) _____. She was sure it was a joke by a neighbor, but I finally convinced her that we had been robbed. The police were great. They took

(5) _____ action and started interviewing the neighbors right away. It must have been a(n)

(6) _____ operation. No one saw anyone near our house. Even the sneaky kid down the

street had a(n) (7) _____. He was visiting his grandmother two states away all the time we

were gone. It was no time to try to (8) _____ usual procedures, so I called the insurance

company to get the paperwork started. I guess I should take my wife's view that possessions are only

(9) _____. In fact, she is such a(n) (10) _____ that she now sees the robbery as a

great chance to redecorate the house.

Word Wise

Collocations

I was *oblivious to* the conflicts that would result when I invited Karl to dinner. During dessert, he asked a *provocative question*, and everyone spent the rest of the evening arguing about whether nude sunbathing should be allowed on our beaches. (Chapter 7)

The river was rising; it was time for *decisive action* or most of the town would be flooded. The citizens quickly banded together to fill the sandbags. (Chapter 8)

Word Pairs

Dissent/Assent: Dissent (Chapter 6) means "to differ in feeling or opinion." Assent (Chapter 8) means "to agree or concur." Sam had to dissent from the majority opinion because he felt the way to slow people down was a new stop sign, not lowering the speed limit. Samantha assented to the plan to lower the speed limit because she agreed with the rest of the council that that was the best way to slow traffic near the school.

Covert/Overt: Covert (Chapter 8) means "concealed; secret," while overt means "open; not concealed." Tim's covert feelings for Leslie were in danger of being revealed when he dropped a love note he had written her but never planned to deliver. Tom was so overt with his feelings that Leslie was embarrassed when he announced his love for her over the loud speaker at school.

Connotations and Denotations

Alibi (Chapter 8): denotation—"an excuse or explanation, especially used to avoid blame." For many, the connotation of alibi is a false explanation, possibly from viewing court cases—real or, more often, fictional—where a person lies about being with a person to protect that person from an accusation.

Optimist (Chapter 8): denotation—"a person who looks on the bright side." When some people think of an optimist, they picture a cheery, positive person. For other people, the word *optimist* connotes a person who doesn't want to face the harsher aspects of life. Which way do you see the optimist?

Interesting Etymologies

Alibi (Chapter 8): comes from Latin *alibi*, meaning "elsewhere." It is a reason a person uses to say they couldn't have committed a crime because he or she was somewhere besides where the crime was committed. It has its roots in the Latin *alius*, or "(an)other," such as in the word alias, meaning "another, or false, name."

Interactive Exercise ||||||||||||||||||||||||||||||||||||||||||||||||||||||||||||||||||||||||

List two situations that could be relevant to each word.

EXAMPLE: *presentiment—not wanting to answer the phone (due to a feeling that the call will bring sad news); deciding not to board an airplane (because of a feeling that something bad will happen)*

1. presentiment

_____   _____

2. circumvent

_____   _____

3. incredulous

_____   _____

4. covert

_____   _____

5. misgiving

_____   _____

6. alibi

_____   _____

7. transitory

_____   _____

8. optimist

_____   _____

9. assent

_____   _____

10. decisive

_____   _____

Conversation Starters

An excellent way to review the vocabulary words and help to make them your own is to use them when you are speaking. Gather three to five friends or classmates, and use one or more of the conversation starters below. Before you begin talking, have each person write down six of the vocabulary words he or she will use during the conversation. Share your lists with each other to check that you did not all pick the same six words. Try to cover all of the words you want to study, whether you are reviewing one, two, or more chapters.

1. What science fiction have you enjoyed, whether it was a book, movie, or television show?

2. Do you think real life is at all like romance novels?

3. Do you think you would make a good detective or private eye? Explain why or why not.

4. What kind of books or stories do you most enjoy reading? What makes this type appeal to you?

Word List

alibi
[al′ ə bī′]
n. an excuse or explanation, especially used to avoid blame

assent
[ə sent′]
v. to agree or concur
n. agreement, as to a proposal

circumvent
[sûr′ kəm vent′; sûr′ kəm vent′]
v. 1. to go around
2. to avoid by cleverness; to elude

covert
[kō′ vərt]
adj. concealed; secret; disguised

decisive
[di sī′ siv]
adj. 1. definite; clear
2. displaying firmness; determined
3. crucial; important

incredulous
[in krej′ ə ləs]
adj. skeptical; doubtful; disbelieving

misgiving
[mis giv′ ing]
n. a feeling of doubt or distrust

optimist
[op′ tə mist]
n. a person who looks on the bright side; one who expects a positive result

presentiment
[pri zen′ tə mənt]
n. a feeling that something is about to happen, especially something bad; foreboding; expectation

transitory
[tran′ si tôr′ ē]
adj. not lasting; temporary

Words to Watch

Which words would you like to practice with a bit more? Pick 3–5 words to study, and list them below. Write the word and its definition, and compose your own sentence using the word correctly. This extra practice could be the final touch to learning a word.

Word	Definition	Your Sentence
1.		
2.		
3.		
4.		
5.		

Word Parts II

Look for words with these **prefixes**, **roots**, and/or **suffixes** as you work through this book. You may have already seen some of them, and you will see others in later chapters. Learning basic word parts can help you figure out the meanings of unfamiliar words.

prefix: a word part added to the beginning of a word that changes the meaning of the root

root: a word's basic part with its essential meaning

suffix: a word part added to the end of a word; indicates the part of speech

Word Part	Meaning	Examples and Definitions
Prefixes		
mis-	wrong	*misconstrue:* to understand wrongly *misgiving:* a feeling that something is wrong
omni-	all	*omnipresent:* present at all places *omniscient:* knowing all
sub-, sup-	below, under	*submerge:* to put below water *suppress:* to keep under control
Roots		
-cred-	to believe, to trust	*credo:* a statement of belief *credentials:* evidence of one's right to be trusted
-pend-, -pens-	to hang, to weigh, to pay	*suspend:* to hang *pensive:* to weigh an idea; thoughtful
-sens-, -sent-	to feel, to be aware	*consensus:* feeling the same way *dissent:* to differ in feeling
-vers-, -vert-	to turn	*versatile:* capable of turning easily from one task to another *avert:* to turn away
Suffixes		
-ism (makes a noun)	action, practice, theory	*voyeurism:* the action of watching others *patriotism:* the practice of loving one's country
-ist (makes a noun)	a person who	*naturalist:* a person who is an expert on plant or animal life *columnist:* a person who writes a column
-ology (makes a noun)	the study of	*zoology:* the study of animals *biology:* the study of life

1 Read each definition, and choose the appropriate word from the list below. Use each word once. The meaning of the word part is underlined to help you make the connection. Refer to the Word Parts list if you need help.

VOCABULARY LIST

astrology	misuse	zoologist	expensive	subterranean
controversy	omnipotent	credible	sensitive	plagiarism

1. to operate the <u>wrong</u> way _____
2. <u>turn</u> against; an argument _____
3. capable of being <u>believed</u> _____
4. the <u>action</u> of using another's words as one's own _____
5. <u>the study of</u> the stars as influences on people's lives _____
6. <u>all</u> -powerful _____
7. <u>paying a lot for</u> _____
8. <u>underground</u> _____
9. <u>a person who</u> studies animals _____
10. <u>aware of the feelings of others</u> _____

2 Finish the sentences with the meaning of each word part. Use each meaning once. The word part is underlined to help you make the connection.

VOCABULARY LIST

below	feels	all	wrong	to turn
practice	the study of	trusts	hanging	a person who

1. A <u>senti</u>mental person _____ strongly about old items.
2. If you make a <u>mis</u>take, you do the _____ thing.
3. When a company gives a person <u>cred</u>it, it _____ that the person will pay his or her bills.
4. A <u>sub</u>ordinate works _____ his or her boss.
5. <u>Rac</u>ism is the _____ of believing one's ethnic background is better than other people's.
6. The child wanted to <u>di</u>vert attention from the mess he had made, so he tried _____ his mother's interest to the sound of a siren out front.
7. The diamond <u>pend</u>ant was _____ around her neck.
8. The <u>omni</u>scient narrator in the novel knew what was happening to _____ the characters.
9. A <u>solo</u>ist is _____ performs alone.
10. I will pursue _____ psycho<u>logy</u> because I enjoy learning about the mind.

3 Finish the story using the word parts below. Use each word part once. Your knowledge of word parts, as well as the context clues, will help you create the correct words. If you do not understand the meaning of a word you have made, check your dictionary for the definition or to see whether the word exists.

WORD PARTS LIST

omni	pend	ist	vert	cred
sup	ism	mis	ology	sent

ALL FIRED UP

My excursion to the art gallery became quite an adventure. While I was looking at a sculpture, a fire alarm sounded. I hurried outside. Lingering out front, I heard a rumor that an arson(1)_____ had started the fire. I have been studying crimin(2)_____, so I began talking with people to find out what was happening. People didn't (3)_____press their opinions. I heard that one of the gallery owners, Pierre, and his wife were having problems. I also discovered that Pierre's business partner had several gambling debts. Problems in Pierre's life seemed to be (4)_____present.

Then I heard a man shout, "*C'est une catastrophe!*" It was Pierre; he was in shock. I told him he could de(5)_____ on me for help because I was going to be an insurance investigator, and I had studied similar cases in college. Pierre con(6)_____ed to my helping him. After the fire was out, we went in to survey the damage. It was in(7)_____ible, but only one painting was seriously damaged. When Pierre began to pick up bits of the frame, I told him to be careful not to disturb any evidence. If we (8)_____handled the situation at the beginning, we would never find what caused the fire. Pierre began to complain that we would never discover who tried to ruin him. Just when his pessim(9)_____ was at its greatest, I noticed wax on a nearby table. Pierre's eyes lit up—he had inad(10)_____ently set a candle there when he had gone to answer the phone. We had found the guilty party.

4 Pick the best definition for each underlined word using your knowledge of word parts. Circle the word part in each of the underlined words.

a. the study of birds

b. to feel angry

c. pay

d. below the required level

e. eating all kinds of food

f. a person who commits blackmail

g. evidence that one is qualified or can be trusted

h. a turning away; hatred

i. the action of putting great value on objects

j. given wrong information

_____ 1. Because Harry's work for the last three months had been substandard, his boss called him in to see what was wrong.

_____ 2. The reporter showed his credentials to gain access to the crime scene.

_____ 3. After a fascinating day of observing condors, vultures, and falcons at the zoo, I may have a future in ornithology.

_____ 4. Omnivorous eaters can satisfy their hunger with plants or animals.

_____ 5. We were misinformed about the meeting. We thought it began at three o'clock, but it really began at two.

_____ 6. I had to spend more than one hundred dollars on dry cleaning last month; I need to get more machine washable clothes.

_____ 7. I have an aversion to getting up early; I could easily sleep until ten o'clock every morning.

_____ 8. I resent that I did all the work while my colleagues got all the credit.

_____ 9. The family's materialism led to financial problems; they couldn't afford everything they bought.

_____10. The extortionist asked for $10,000 to be delivered by noon the next day or he would reveal the mayor's secret.

5 A good way to remember word parts is to pick one word that uses a word part and understand how that word part functions in the word. Then you can apply that meaning to other words that have the same word part. Use the following words to help you match the word part to its meaning.

Set One

_____ 1. **mis-**: misgivings, mislead, mistake

_____ 2. **sub-, sup-**: submerge, submissive, suppress

_____ 3. **cred-**: credibility, incredible, credit

_____ 4. **-ology**: zoology, biology, psychology

_____ 5. **-sens-, -sent-**: consensus, sentimental, dissent

a. the study of

b. to feel, to be aware

c. below, under

d. wrong

e. to believe, to trust

Set Two

_____ 6. **omni-**: omniscient, omnipresent, omnipotent

_____ 7. **-vers-, -vert-**: aversion, covert, avert

_____ 8. **-ist**: naturalist, arsonist, artist

_____ 9. **-pend-, -pens-**: suspend, pendant, pensive

_____10. **-ism**: patriotism, pessimism, humanism

f. a person who

g. all

h. action, practice, theory

i. to turn

j. to hang, to weigh, to pay

Interactive Exercise |||||||||||||||||||||||||||||||||||||||||||||||||||||||||||||||||||||||||||||||||||

Use the dictionary to find a word you don't know that uses each word part listed below. Write the meaning of the word part, the word, and the definition. If your dictionary has the etymology (history) of the word, see how the word part relates to the meaning, and write the etymology after the definition.

Word Part	Meaning	Word	Definition and Etymology
EXAMPLE:			
-pend-	to hang	pendulous	1. hanging loosely
			2. undecided
			Latin "pendulus," from "pendēre," to hang
1. sub-			
2. mis-			
3. omni-			
4. -cred-			
5. -sent-			

Word Wise

A Different Approach: Word Groups

Putting words into related groups can be a way to help your mind organize new vocabulary. To create word groups, get a piece of paper, pick a category, and list as many of the vocabulary words whose definitions fit under that heading in a general way. You will, of course, need to know the shades of meaning the more frequently you use a word.

Here is a sample list of vocabulary words that fit the definition of "hidden or secret": *clandestine* and *intrigue* (Chapter 3), *covert* (Chapter 8), *circumspection* (Chapter 13), and *façade* (Chapter 18). As you work through the book, look for five other words that would fit this category, and return here to complete the list.

1. _____

2. _____

3. _____

4. _____

5. _____

A few other categories to use for the vocabulary words in this text are "free/freedom," "cheat," and "excitement." For a fun and collaborative way to use word groups, see the directions for Category Race in Chapter 16.

HINT

Tips for Enjoying a Novel or Short Story

Readers enjoy a book more when they become involved with it. Try to put yourself in the novel or short story by imagining yourself in a character's situation. What would you do if you had to stop an alien invasion, cope with a broken heart, or solve a murder? Learn to appreciate the descriptions of the places in the story. Try to visualize yourself hiking through the jungle, cooking a big meal in the kitchen, or hiding under a bed. Look for the author's message as you read. Ask yourself what point the author is trying to get across. Do you agree or disagree with the author's point? By putting yourself in the story and thinking about the significance of events, you will want to keep reading to see what happens to the characters because now they and their world are a part of you.

Focus on Chapters 6–9

The following activities give you a chance to interact some more with the vocabulary words you've learned. By looking at art, taking tests, answering questions, doing a crossword puzzle, and working with others, you will see which words you know well and which you still need to work with.

Art

Match each picture below to one of the following vocabulary words. Use each word once.

VOCABULARY LIST

subjugate	seclusion	dissent
transitory	covert	virile

1. _____

2. _____

3. _____

4. _____

5. _____

6. _____

Self-Tests

1 Pick the word that best completes each sentence.

1. The battle was a(n) _____ one; the next day the enemy surrendered.

   a. incredulous   b. oblivious   c. decisive   d. cursory

2. It is easy to see how much Anita _____ housework because dust covers all her furniture.

   a. abhors   b. condones   c. assents   d. subjugates

3. The king considered himself _____ until the ruler in the next kingdom sent ten thousand knights into battle against him.

   a. cursory   b. amorous   c. covert   d. omnipotent

4. The man stayed _____ through daily exercise and a healthy diet.

   a. precise   b. provocative   c. transitory   d. virile

5. An accountant needs to be _____. There can be big problems if the numbers don't add up correctly.

   a. omnipotent   b. covert   c. precise   d. virile

2 Pick the vocabulary word that best completes the sentence. Use each word once.

a. pandemonium	b. alibi	c. seclusion	d. optimist	e. dissent

1. Lance didn't have a good _____. The restaurant he said he had been at the night of the robbery was closed for repairs at the time.

2. After having guests for two weeks, I was looking forward to a bit of _____ at my mountain cabin.

3. There was a lot of _____ at the meeting over raising the dues $100 to cover the cost of adding a new parking area.

4. I was shocked at the _____ in the classroom when I returned. I had only run across the hall to borrow chalk from another teacher, and the classroom was in chaos when I returned.

5. I like traveling with Eileen because she is such a(n) _____. No matter what goes wrong, she is able to find a bright side to it.

3 Finish the story using the vocabulary words below. Use each word once.

VOCABULARY LIST

amorous	assent	misgivings	covert	cursory
delude	oblivious	miscalculated	condone	transitory

A WINTER PLAN

I had some (1)_____ when my girlfriend called and wanted me to come over just as the snowstorm was beginning. She said she was feeling lonely and (2)_____. I hated to disappoint her. I took a(n) (3)_____ look outside. From my peak out the window, I didn't think it looked too bad yet. It is easy to (4)_____ oneself when love is involved. All of a sudden I became (5)_____ to the possible dangers of traveling on icy roads or trying to get through streets covered with snow. I knew none of my friends would (6)_____ such reckless behavior, so I didn't call anyone to say where I was going. This was going to be my (7)_____ operation of love.

Just as I was tying my boots, the phone rang again. It was my girlfriend calling to say that she had (8)_____ the strength of the storm, and she didn't think I should come. I protested at first, but I finally had to (9)_____ when I saw that she was right about endangering my life. She told me that her love for me wasn't (10)_____ but that bad weather was. We would be together again in just a couple of days.

Interactive Exercise ||||||||||||||||||||||||||||||||||||||||||||||||||||||||||||||||||||||||||||||||||||||||||||||||||||

Answer the following questions to further test your understanding of the vocabulary words.

1. What procedure would you like to circumvent? Why?

_____

_____

2. What are two methods people have used to subjugate other people?

_____

_____

3. What do you have an antipathy toward?

_____

_____

4. How might someone embellish a story about a game or contest he or she was in?

_____

_____

5. Give an example of a statement you would be incredulous about.

_____

_____

6. What is something you have had a presentiment about?

_____

_____

7. Where would you like to be sent as an emissary? Why would you like to go there?

_____

_____

8. What are two kinds of experiences that can cause euphoria?

_____

_____

9. What is something you would like to annihilate? Why?

_____

_____

10. What is a provocative question you could ask at the dinner table?

_____

_____

Crossword Puzzle

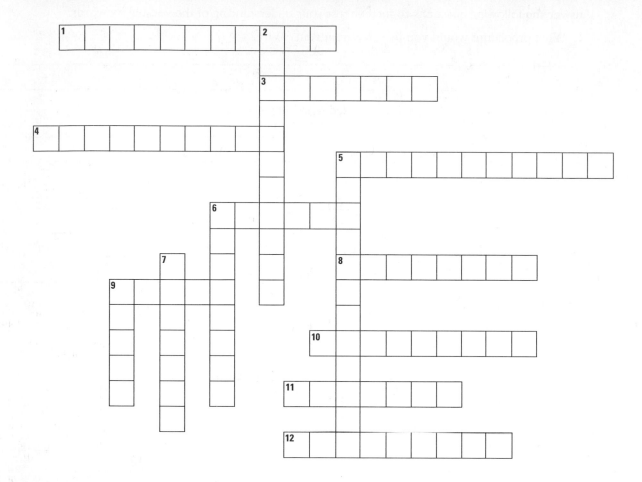

Use the following words to complete the crossword puzzle. Use each word once.

VOCABULARY LIST

abhor	euphoria
alibi	incredulous
annihilate	misgiving
antipathy	pandemonium
cursory	precise
decisive	presentiment
delude	provocative
dissent	

Across

1. stimulating
3. hasty
4. to destroy
5. disorder; chaos
6. to mislead
8. feeling one should have on one's wedding day
9. I was with three friends all night.
10. a feeling of distrust
11. accurate or demanding
12. an aversion

Down

2. I don't believe your story.
5. foreboding
6. displaying firmness
7. I don't feel the same way.
9. I hate that style.

HINT

Read for Fun

It might sound obvious, but many people forget that reading for fun makes you a better reader overall. If you think you don't like to read, search for reading material about a subject that interests you. Textbooks are not always the most exciting reading material, so don't give up if you don't enjoy what you currently have to read.

Assess your reading interests:

- Do you like to keep up on current events? Become a newspaper or weekly newsmagazine reader.
- Do you have a hobby? Subscribe to a magazine on the topic.
- Do you like to look into people's lives? Pick up a collection of short stories or a novel. You can find everything from romance to mystery in fiction writing.
- Is there a time period you are interested in? Nonfiction and fiction books deal with events from the days of the dinosaurs to the unknown future.
- Are you interested in travel or different countries? Try books by authors from foreign lands.
- Do you like to read in short spurts or for long periods? Newspaper articles, essays, poetry, and short stories may appeal more to those who like to read a little at a time. Novels, plays, and nonfiction books may appeal more to those who like intricate tales.

Visit the library to try out different types of reading material. It's free! Also explore the Internet for various reading sources.

Finding the type of reading material that is right for your personality and interests will make reading fun, will lead to better reading skills, and will even make the reading you are required to do more productive.

Mix It Up

Making a Scene

Get together with six to nine classmates and divide into two to three groups. Each group creates a situation or uses one of the suggestions below to write a short scene using at least six of the vocabulary words to be studied. If you want to study several words, make sure each group doesn't pick the same six words. Each group acts out the scene with the rest noting how the words are used. You may choose to emphasize the vocabulary word by your actions or tone of voice when you are doing the scene to help you and your classmates remember the word. Discuss how the words fit in after the scene is completed. The scenes can also be done as role-playing with pairs creating the scenes instead of small groups. The scenes might be from the readings, such as two people eating out from Chapter 3. Creating scenes is an especially fun and useful activity if you like to act or enjoy movement.

The following are possible scenes related to specific chapters: crewmates discussing their new mission from Chapter 6, Estella's neighbors talking about all the noise at her place the night before from Chapter 7, and the baseball team in the locker room wondering where Thompson is just before the game is about to begin from Chapter 8. You can also use the overall section theme of Reading for Pleasure to create your own ideas using words from all three chapters.

If you enjoy this collaborative activity, remember to use it again when you are reviewing later chapters in this book. Have fun making the scenes, and you will enjoy the review process.

PART II Academic Words

Page 72

Page 78

Page 108

Creating Readers

Reading Is Essential

Reading is one of the essential skills in this world, and parents or other adults can **nurture** that skill in children. The easiest way to **facilitate** reading development in children is to read to them aloud. When parents, grandparents, aunts, uncles, or neighbors take the time to read to children, children become interested in the reading process. Reading aloud to children can begin at a very young age, even within weeks of birth. Most experts recommend that parents **adhere** to at least a half hour a day of reading to a child to develop an interest in reading. Children hear new vocabulary when they are read to, and that stimulates the brain. A child's language skills can even **surpass** adult expectations when discussion of a book becomes part of the reading environment. When adults talk to children about the stories they

have read together—what happened, which characters they liked best, what the point of the story was—children's critical thinking skills are greatly increased.

Adults shouldn't **impose** their reading interests or level on a child. Asking children to read books too far above their comprehension level can **impede** their reading development. The mastery of reading is tied to self-esteem, so parents want to make sure not to push their children. A simple way to see if a child wants to read a book is to take the child to the library or bookstore and let the child find books that interest him or her. An adult can guide a child's choices, especially based on the child's interests (dinosaurs, knights, the ocean), but the child should be excited about the books the family takes home to read. Children have an **innate** interest in language, and parents can support that natural interest through wise reading choices.

Parents can also be reading **advocates** by having books in the home and reading themselves. When a child sees a parent enjoy reading, the child learns that it is a fun and important skill to acquire. Today's children are so **susceptible** to the lure of television and video games (most children spend three to four hours a day in front of the television) that it is essential for parents to take the lead in making reading an exciting and memorable experience. All children have the **potential** to be successful readers. For some children, reading skills will come quickly and easily; for others, it will take more time. If parents are ever unsure about a child's reading ability, they can always contact school or community programs for advice.

Predicting

For each set, write the definition on the line next to the word to which it belongs. If you are unsure, return to the reading on page 72, and underline any context clues you find. After you've made your predictions, check your answers against the Word List on page 77. Place a checkmark in the box next to each word whose definition you missed. These are the words you'll want to study closely.

Set One

to force on others	to make easier	to educate or train	to go beyond	to follow closely

☐ 1. **nurture** (line 2) _____

☐ 2. **facilitate** (line 4) _____

☐ 3. **adhere** (line 11) _____

☐ 4. **surpass** (line 15) _____

☐ 5. **impose** (line 23) _____

Set Two

to block	supporters of a cause	open to an influence	the ability for development	possessed at birth

☐ 6. **impede** (line 26) _____

☐ 7. **innate** (line 37) _____

☐ 8. **advocates** (line 40) _____

☐ 9. **susceptible** (line 45) _____

☐ 10. **potential** (line 50) _____

Self-Tests

1 In each group, there are three synonyms and one antonym. Circle the antonym.

1. impede	block	facilitate	obstruct
2. urge	oppose	advocate	recommend
3. force	impose	require	choose
4. develop	educate	hinder	nurture
5. assist	impede	help	facilitate
6. release	adhere	stick	hold
7. exceed	surpass	fail	excel
8. natural	learned	inborn	innate
9. possible	unlikely	budding	potential
10. resistant	exposed	sensitive	susceptible

2 Finish the readings using the vocabulary words. Use each word once.

VOCABULARY LIST

impose	adhere	innate	impedes	potential
facilitates	surpassed	susceptible	advocate	nurtured

SET ONE

I (1)_____ to a steady reading plan. I get three books from the library every other week. My parents (2)_____ my love of reading when I was young. Every summer they would sign me up for the library's reading program. If I read ten books, I got a prize. Sometimes work (3)_____ my reading plan. I get busy with a project or come home so tired that I don't feel like reading. But those times are rare. I love to read, and having the library so close really (4)_____ my reading habit. There are so many great books there to choose from. I am such a(n) (5)_____ for the library that I have started volunteering to read during story time once a week. This week the kids get to hear *Penguin on the Lookout*. It is one of my favorites.

SET TWO

I loved school, though I was (6)_____ to colds and missed more days than I wanted to. I discovered I had a(n) (7)_____ talent for drawing in the second grade. I continued to do sketches of friends throughout school, and I enjoyed using watercolors in college. I minored in art, but I didn't think I really had the (8)_____ to become a famous artist. I didn't want to (9)_____ on my friends and family while I struggled to make it in the art world. Instead I (10)_____ my parents' expectations and went into medicine. In the field of medical research, I still get to draw sometimes, and maybe someday I can find a cure for the common cold so kids won't have to miss school like I did.

3 Complete the sentences using the vocabulary words. Use each word once.

VOCABULARY LIST

impeded	innate	susceptible	surpassed	facilitate
nurture	adhere	advocate	imposed	potential

1. I _____ to the idea of saving money for a happier future.

2. My _____ talents are in music and dance; I have always done well in those areas.

3. I have the _____ to do well in all my classes if I take the time to study.

4. To _____ the moving process, I clearly labeled all the boxes.

5. The _____ appeared on the talk show to explain his views on why we need more land for parks.

6. I hope to _____ a love of reading in my children by reading a story to them every night before bed.

7. The reading selections in my literature class have _____ my expectations: they are all fascinating.

8. My parents _____ a ten o'clock curfew on me when I was in high school.

9. Because I am _____ to illness, I like to wear a sweater when it is chilly.

10. Our plans were _____ by the rainy weather. We had to wait until the sun came out to have our picnic.

Word Wise

Context Clue Mini-Lesson 3

This lesson uses examples to explain the unknown word. The example may consist of one illustration of the word or be a list of items. In the paragraph below, circle the examples you find that clarify the meaning of the underlined words. Then use the examples to write your own definitions on the lines next to the words that follow the paragraph.

The hotel was palatial with its spacious rooms, private hot tubs, balconies with ocean views, four swimming pools, three restaurants, and a disco. I couldn't believe I had won a free weekend. I enjoyed my afternoon repast of lobster, fresh fruit, a variety of salads, and chocolate cake. Now it was time for a relaxing nap. However, the incessant noise from outside began to bother me. Within twenty minutes of closing my eyes, music blared from the disco, a dog started barking, and a large group of people settled outside my window to chat. I was not going to let these annoyances infringe on my vacation, like I let Uncle Stephan do last year when we went fishing and he complained the whole time about the cold water. I decided my wisest move was to take a walk in the lovely garden and relax that way.

Your Definition

1. Palatial _____

2. Repast _____

3. Incessant _____

4. Infringe _____

Interactive Exercise

Write a letter to a favorite teacher thanking him or her for inspiring or helping you (pick a teacher from elementary school to college). Once you have drafted your letter below, consider recopying the letter and actually sending or giving it to the teacher. Teachers love to hear from former students. Use at least six of the vocabulary words in your letter.

Dear _____,

_____

_____

_____

_____

_____

_____

_____

_____

_____

_____

_____

Sincerely,

_____

Word Part Reminder

Below are a few short exercises to help you review the word parts you have been learning. Fill in the missing word part from the list, and circle the meaning of the word part found in each sentence. Try to complete the questions without returning to the Word Parts chapter, but if you get stuck, look back at Chapter 9.

| sent | mis | ist | pens |

1. My cousin is a person who loves music, so I suggested he become a pian_____.

2. My father said he was surprised to feel the same way I did, but because he supported the campaign to build a community center, he gave his con_____ for me to stay out after ten o'clock to help at the fundraiser.

3. Suzy doesn't usually do anything wrong when I babysit her, but today she was in a mood to _____behave.

4. It was more than I wanted to pay; I thought $50 was too ex_____ive for a ripped poster even if it was of my favorite band.

Word List

adhere
[ad hēr']

v. 1. to follow closely
2. to give support
3. to stick together

advocate
n. [ad' və kit, -kāt']
v. [ad' və kāt']

n. a person who supports a cause
v. to support or urge; to recommend

facilitate
[fə sil' ə tāt']

v. to make easier; to assist

impede
[im pēd']

v. to block; to hinder

impose
[im pōz']

v. to force on others

innate
[i nāt', in' āt]

adj. 1. possessed at birth
2. possessed as an essential characteristic

nurture
[nûr' chər]

v. to educate or train
n. the act of promoting development or growth; rearing

potential
[pə ten' shəl]

n. the ability for growth or development
adj. possible but not yet realized

surpass
[sər pas']

v. to go beyond; to excel; to be superior to

susceptible
[sə sep' tə bəl]

adj. open to an influence; sensitive

Words to Watch

Which words would you like to practice with a bit more? Pick 3–5 words to study, and list them below. Write the word and its definition, and compose your own sentence using the word correctly. This extra practice could be the final touch to learning a word.

Word	Definition	Your Sentence
1.		
2.		
3.		
4.		
5.		

12 Environmental Science

Endangered Animals

The International Union for the Conservation of Nature and Natural Resources (IUCN) has a list of endangered plants and animals known as the Red List. Animals on the list range from the well-known lowland gorilla to the lesser known aye-aye. Within the "threatened" category, animals are listed as "critically endangered," "endangered," or "vulnerable." The 2007 list puts 7,850 animals worldwide in
5 the threatened category. **Conservationists** hope the list will heighten public awareness of the dangers animals face and **elicit** responses on ways to save these animals.

The giant panda, a symbol for endangered animals, is **endemic** to Southwest China. The panda eats about twenty to
10 thirty pounds of bamboo a day. As human populations grow, animals lose more of their natural **habitat**. Forests and grasslands are being destroyed for timber, agriculture, and housing expansion. The giant panda's habitat is diminishing due to **encroachment** for agriculture and timber needs. The Chinese
15 government has established more than fifty panda reserves, which shields almost 60 percent of the current population. Estimates place about 1,600 pandas in the wild.

The babirusa, or wild pig, found on Sulawesi and other Indonesian islands is listed as vulnerable. The unusual-looking
20 babirusa has two sets of tusks, one of which grows on the top of the snout and curves back toward the animal's forehead. The babirusa is **omnivorous**, eating fruit, leaves, and small animals. Though protected, hunting contributes to the animal's decline. They are killed for food, and their unusual skulls are found in local markets for sale to tourists. In the last census, only 5,000 babirusa were found in the wild.

25   The blue whale, found in every ocean, is listed as endangered. The largest **mammal** on Earth, blue whales are usually 80 to 100 feet long and weigh more than 100 tons. They eat about 8,000 pounds a day of krill, a shrimp-like animal. Before the whaling era, population estimates were 350,000 animals. About
30 99 percent were killed due to whaling. In 1966, the International Whaling Commission put a **moratorium** on hunting blue whales. By 2002, estimates placed the blue whale population between 5,000 and 12,000. Blue whales now face threats from pollution, including increases in ocean noise levels (possibly interfering with
35 their low-frequency communication) and global warming (disrupting migration patterns and altering food supplies).

These examples illustrate the major threats animals face: habitat loss, hunting, and pollution. The field of **zoology** has helped people learn more about animals. With this knowledge and
40 by working together, individuals and governments can **avert** the loss of today's threatened animals.

Predicting

For each set, write the definition on the line next to the word to which it belongs. If you are unsure, return to the reading on page 78, and underline any context clues you find. After you've made your predictions, check your answers against the Word List on page 83. Place a checkmark in the box next to each word whose definition you missed. These are the words you'll want to study closely.

Set One

to draw or bring out	an intrusion	the environment where a plant or animal typically lives
natural to a particular area	a person who works to save the environment	

☐ 1. **conservationist** (line 5) _____

☐ 2. **elicit** (line 6) _____

☐ 3. **endemic** (line 9) _____

☐ 4. **habitat** (line 11) _____

☐ 5. **encroachment** (line 14) _____

Set Two

suspension of an activity	to prevent	warm-blooded vertebrate	the study of animals
eating all types of food			

☐ 6. **omnivorous** (line 21) _____

☐ 7. **mammal** (line 26) _____

☐ 8. **moratorium** (line 31) _____

☐ 9. **zoology** (line 38) _____

☐ 10. **avert** (line 40) _____

Self-Tests

1 Write the appropriate vocabulary word next to each sentence. Context clues are underlined to help you. Use each word once.

VOCABULARY LIST

habitat	endemic	mammals	elicit	encroachment
omnivorous	zoology	conservationist	moratorium	avert

1. They have been ordered to stop dumping waste there. _____
2. Africa has lots of these, including lions, elephants, and zebras. _____
3. Charles is interested in studying animals. _____
4. It was only when I mentioned dinner that I was able to get a response from my kids. _____

5. The city has slowly been growing into the hills, and cougars have recently been seen in people's back yards. _____

6. Orangutans are at home in the forest, swinging from tree to tree. _____

7. We turned away from Main Street minutes before the crane fell. We were lucky to miss the accident. _____

8. Chimpanzees eat leaves, fruit, insects, birds, and small mammals. _____

9. The saguaro cactus is found only in the Southwest. _____

10. Grandpa belongs to a group that spends two weekends a month removing nonnative plants from local parks. _____

2 Fill in each blank with the appropriate vocabulary word. Use each word once.

SET ONE

Henry was surprised that seeing a blue whale would (1)_____ so many emotions from him. He was happy, sad, and amazed. He had been told that they are the world's largest (2)_____ (as long as three school buses), but he hadn't really comprehended that until he saw one in person. He was so impressed that he wanted to do something to (3)_____ their disappearance. It was on that day that Henry became a(n) (4)_____. Now he writes letters, sends money, and works with local groups to preserve the (5)_____ of endangered animals in the forests, grasslands, and oceans around the globe.

SET TWO

One of the endangered animals Henry learned about is the aye-aye. It is a primate that is (6)_____ to Madagascar. It eats fruits, nuts, seeds, and grubs, which makes it (7)_____.

Due to (8) _____ of its rainforest habitat, aye-aye have been found more often raiding local villages for food. There is local superstition that the aye-aye is an omen of evil and that it sneaks into people's homes and kills them with its long middle finger. Because of these beliefs, aye-aye are often killed by locals. The story of the aye-aye fascinated Henry and encouraged him to take a(n) (9) _____ course at his local college. As Henry says, "there should never be a(n) (10) _____ on learning."

3 Use the vocabulary words to complete the following analogies. For more instructions, see Completing Analogies on page 6.

VOCABULARY LIST

avert	endemic	zoology	elicit	omnivorous
habitat	mammal	encroachment	conservationist	moratorium

1. New Orleans : city :: rainforest : _____
2. new : old :: beginning : _____
3. cook : makes food :: _____ : works to save the environment
4. examine : study :: _____ : prevent
5. oak : tree :: giraffe : _____
6. pots and pans : cooking :: questions : _____
7. looks both ways before crossing the street : cautious :: eats fruit and animals : _____
8. steering wheel : car :: clearing away trees : _____
9. mailed : sent :: _____ : native
10. write a letter : mail it :: want to learn about animals : study _____

Word Wise

Internet Activity: For Further Study

When you get the urge to expand your vocabulary knowledge online, try visiting some of the sites below.

- For a list of challenging words, several of which you are learning in this text, and how many times a word has appeared in the *New York Times* in the last year with an example of the word in context, visit www.nytimes.com/learning/students/wordofday.

- For dictionary entries, a word of the day feature, and word-related games, give the Merriam-Webster online dictionary a look at www.m-w.com.

- For a list of more Web sites related to vocabulary study, refer to the back cover of this text.

Enjoy exploring the Internet's many resources, but watch your time. It can be easy to lose track of time as you link from one site to the next.

Interactive Exercise

Interview a Conservationist

Prepare for an imaginary interview with a conservationist by writing five questions that you could ask the person. Use at least five vocabulary words in your questions.

Sample Questions:

1. What are some types of animals that are endemic to this part of the country?

2. What can I do to stop encroachment in my state?

Your Questions:

1. _____
2. _____
3. _____
4. _____
5. _____

HINT

Study Groups

A class can be more rewarding if you find classmates to study with. To create effective study groups, keep these points in mind.

- Get people who really want to learn, not just socialize.
- Have everyone who is interested in the group write out a weekly schedule with class times, work schedules, family obligations, and the best times to meet.
- Pick a time that can accommodate most people; it may be impossible to get everyone together all the time.
- Decide how often you will meet—twice a week, once a week, every other week.
- Find out whether the group members like to eat while studying—it will influence the study place.
- Pick a place that promotes studying. See whether the library has study group rooms. You want a place where you can talk freely and where you won't be interrupted by the telephone, children, or other distractions.
- Bring the necessary books, notes, and other materials to each session.
- Ask group members to be "the expert" on different chapters or areas of study—have them share their in-depth study with the other group members.
- Assign someone to keep the group on track and to remind the members, if people start to talk about other topics, that you are all there to study. Ask anyone to leave who does not really want to study.
- Evaluate how useful each study session is and decide what changes may be needed for the next time.

Word List

avert
[ə vûrt′]

v. 1. to prevent
2. to turn away or aside

conservationist
[kon′ sûr vā′ shə nist]

n. a person who works to save the environment; an environmentalist

elicit
[i lis′ it]

v. to draw or bring out; to obtain

encroachment
[en krōch′ mənt]

n. the act of gradually taking over an area or possessions that belong to someone else; an intrusion

endemic
[en dem′ ik]

adj. natural to a particular area; native

habitat
[hab′ i tat′]

n. 1. the environment where a plant or animal typically lives; surroundings
2. the place where something or someone is usually found

mammal
[mam′ əl]

n. warm-blooded vertebrate (animal with a backbone)

moratorium
[môr ə tôr′ ē əm]

n. suspension of an activity; an end or halt

omnivorous
[om niv′ ər əs]

adj. eating all types of food

zoology
[zō ol′ ə jē]

n. the study of animals, including their behavior and development

Words to Watch

Which words would you like to practice with a bit more? Pick 3–5 words to study, and list them below. Write the word and its definition, and compose your own sentence using the word correctly. This extra practice could be the final touch to learning a word.

Word	Definition	Your Sentence
1. _____	_____	_____
2. _____	_____	_____
3. _____	_____	_____
4. _____	_____	_____
5. _____	_____	_____

Chapter
13 Computer Science

Internet Scams

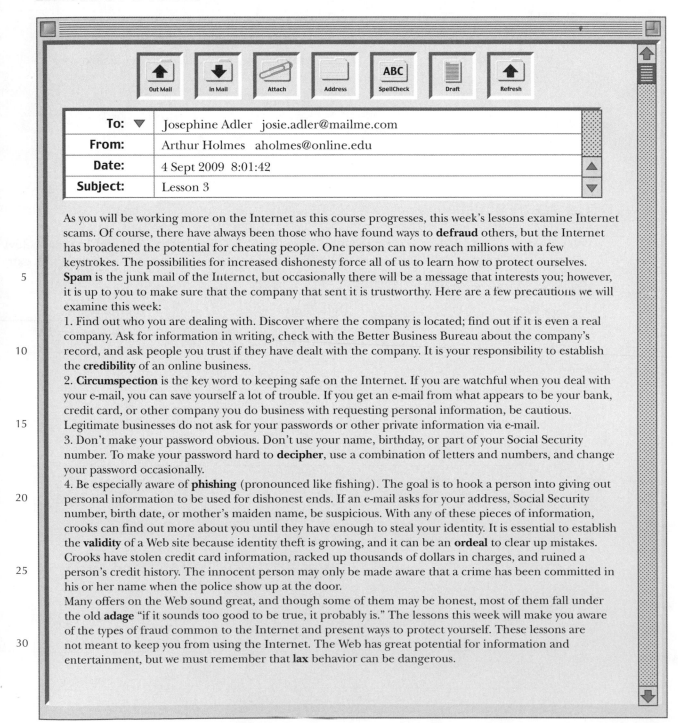

To: ▼	Josephine Adler josie.adler@mailme.com
From:	Arthur Holmes aholmes@online.edu
Date:	4 Sept 2009 8:01:42
Subject:	Lesson 3

As you will be working more on the Internet as this course progresses, this week's lessons examine Internet scams. Of course, there have always been those who have found ways to **defraud** others, but the Internet has broadened the potential for cheating people. One person can now reach millions with a few keystrokes. The possibilities for increased dishonesty force all of us to learn how to protect ourselves.

5 **Spam** is the junk mail of the Internet, but occasionally there will be a message that interests you; however, it is up to you to make sure that the company that sent it is trustworthy. Here are a few precautions we will examine this week:

1. Find out who you are dealing with. Discover where the company is located; find out if it is even a real company. Ask for information in writing, check with the Better Business Bureau about the company's

10 record, and ask people you trust if they have dealt with the company. It is your responsibility to establish the **credibility** of an online business.

2. **Circumspection** is the key word to keeping safe on the Internet. If you are watchful when you deal with your e-mail, you can save yourself a lot of trouble. If you get an e-mail from what appears to be your bank, credit card, or other company you do business with requesting personal information, be cautious.

15 Legitimate businesses do not ask for your passwords or other private information via e-mail.

3. Don't make your password obvious. Don't use your name, birthday, or part of your Social Security number. To make your password hard to **decipher**, use a combination of letters and numbers, and change your password occasionally.

4. Be especially aware of **phishing** (pronounced like fishing). The goal is to hook a person into giving out

20 personal information to be used for dishonest ends. If an e-mail asks for your address, Social Security number, birth date, or mother's maiden name, be suspicious. With any of these pieces of information, crooks can find out more about you until they have enough to steal your identity. It is essential to establish the **validity** of a Web site because identity theft is growing, and it can be an **ordeal** to clear up mistakes. Crooks have stolen credit card information, racked up thousands of dollars in charges, and ruined a

25 person's credit history. The innocent person may only be made aware that a crime has been committed in his or her name when the police show up at the door.

Many offers on the Web sound great, and though some of them may be honest, most of them fall under the old **adage** "if it sounds too good to be true, it probably is." The lessons this week will make you aware of the types of fraud common to the Internet and present ways to protect yourself. These lessons are

30 not meant to keep you from using the Internet. The Web has great potential for information and entertainment, but we must remember that **lax** behavior can be dangerous.

Predicting

For each set, write the definition on the line next to the word to which it belongs. If you are unsure, return to the reading on page 84, and underline any context clues you find. After you've made your predictions, check your answers against the Word List on page 89. Place a checkmark in the box next to each word whose definition you missed. These are the words you'll want to study closely.

Set One

watchfulness	to cheat	trustworthiness	junk e-mail	to decode

❑ 1. **defraud** (line 2) _____

❑ 2. **spam** (line 5) _____

❑ 3. **credibility** (line 11) _____

❑ 4. **circumspection** (line 12) _____

❑ 5. **decipher** (line 17) _____

Set Two

authenticity	a traditional saying	a trying experience	careless

the practice of luring Internet users to a fake Web site to steal personal information

❑ 6. **phishing** (line 19) _____

❑ 7. **validity** (line 23) _____

❑ 8. **ordeal** (line 23) _____

❑ 9 **adage** (line 28) _____

❑ 10. **lax** (line 31) _____

Self-Tests

1 Put a T for true or F for false next to each sentence.

_____ 1. Those involved in phishing are honest people.

_____ 2. It is easy for most people to decipher hieroglyphics.

_____ 3. Planning a wedding can be an ordeal.

_____ 4. Most people like getting spam in their e-mail.

_____ 5. A mechanic should be lax when repairing a car.

_____ 6. When planning a surprise party, it can be helpful to use circumspection.

_____ 7. If a person is going to buy diamonds, he or she should check the credibility of a store before making a purchase.

_____ 8. It is important to check the validity of a medicine's claims before taking it.

_____ 9. Most parents try to defraud their children out of their allowances.

_____ 10. The adage "The early bird catches the worm" would appeal to most late-sleepers.

2 Answer the following questions using the vocabulary words. Use each word once.

VOCABULARY LIST

| adage | ordeal | circumspection | lax | phishing |
| credibility | defraud | decipher | validity | spam |

1. What has Matthew been _____ about security if he gets a virus on his computer?
   _____

2. If a person offers to sell you a new car for two hundred dollars, what can you assume the person is trying to do to you?
   _____

3. Zora couldn't read the note from her brother because he had written it as he hurried out the door. What couldn't she do?
   _____

4. Toshi carefully read the contract when he signed with a baseball team. What did he want to check? _____

5. What is "The bigger they are, the harder they fall"? _____

6. What would most people call spending a night on the floor of an airport and not having eaten for sixteen hours? _____

7. When trying to find the appropriate birthday present, Colleen carefully asked Suzy about some of her favorite things. What was Colleen using? _____

8. Danny checked out several investment firms before giving one his money. What did he want to make sure about each company? _____

9. If you get an e-mail that appears to be from your credit card company but asks for your password, what is someone doing? _____

10. The company sent out thousands of e-mails to announce their new product. What did they do to people? _____

3 Complete the sentences using the vocabulary words. Use each word once.

VOCABULARY LIST

| spam | validity | phishing | ordeal | decipher |
| lax | adage | defraud | credibility | circumspection |

1. People try to _____ others by stealing their credit card numbers.

2. A detective needs to use _____ when he or she is following someone.

3. The _____ of the witness was called into question when it was discovered the man had been engaged to the suspect in college. It wasn't clear whether he still loved her.

4. I write my notes neatly so I can _____ them when studying for an exam.

5. Traveling to see my aunt is a(n) _____ in the winter; she lives on a dirt road, and it becomes a huge mud pit after even a little rain.

6. I thought I was being careful, but I became a victim of _____. I gave out my Social Security number on a Web site that I thought belonged to my bank.

7. I hate getting _____ in my inbox. I have to delete three to four junk messages each day.

8. I doubted the _____ of Warren's statement that it was snowing outside. Snow seemed unlikely on a July day in Los Angeles.

9. My _____ study habits caused me to fail two of my midterms. I wasn't as careless the rest of the term.

10. I agree with the _____ "Don't count your chickens before they're hatched." You can never be sure about a situation until it is over.

Word Wise

Collocations

The college *adheres to* a strict no-drug policy; anyone caught with illegal drugs on campus will be expelled. (Chapter 11)

The man's mission seemed to be to *impede progress* on the new library; he objected to every aspect of the plan. (Chapter 11)

With an especially hot summer, the city council decided to put a *moratorium on* selling fireworks this year. They could not risk the chance of fires. (Chapter 12)

Lily could not *face the ordeal* of another Thanksgiving at her aunt's house; ten screaming children and eleven cats were too much for her to take. (Chapter 13)

Interesting Etymologies

Ordeal (Chapter 13): comes from a medieval form of trial. If a court could not decide a person's guilt or innocence using the evidence presented, the person had to undergo an *ordal*, meaning "judgment." The person was subjected to a cruel physical test such as putting one's hand in boiling water. If the person showed no injuries after three days, he or she was found innocent. Today an ordeal is "a harsh or trying test or experience," but it is no longer forced on one by the courts.

Spam (Chapter 13): the food product got its name in 1937 from its main ingredient "sp(iced) (h)am." The meaning of "junk e-mail" came in the early 1990s. It is likely taken from a skit done on the British television series *Monty Python's Flying Circus* (1970s) where a restaurant's menu extensively features the food product Spam. In the skit, the word *spam* is repeated continuously, just as spam e-mail is sent again and again.

Interactive Exercise ||||||||||||||||||||||||||||||||||||||||||||||||||||||||||||||||||||||||||||||||||||

Answer the following questions about computers and the Internet.

1. What is one way you can check the validity of a Web site? _____

_____

2. How much spam do you usually get in your e-mail inbox in a day? _____

3. What kind of statement in a spam e-mail would you want to check the credibility of before you considered buying the product advertised?

_____

4. When you first started using a computer, did you find it an ordeal or a pleasure? Explain why.

_____

_____

5. Think of a situation when circumspection would be especially important to use on the Internet.

_____

6. What can you do to protect yourself from phishing? _____

_____

7. What is one way someone might try to defraud you on the Internet? _____

_____

8. What is one reason a person shouldn't be lax when on the Internet? _____

_____

9. Do you find it hard to decipher instructions when you do something on the computer? Give an example of a time it was difficult, or explain why you don't have problems with computers.

_____

_____

10. What is an adage that could apply to using computers? _____

_____

HINT

A World of Words

Keep your eyes open for new words. You will certainly encounter new words in the textbooks you read in college and in the lectures your professors give, but new words can be found everywhere. Don't turn off your learning when you leave the classroom. When you see a new word in the newspaper, on a billboard, or on a poster downtown, use the strategies you have learned in this book: look for context clues around the new word, try to predict the meaning, and check the dictionary if you aren't sure of the meaning. No matter where you are or at what age you may be, your vocabulary can continue to grow.

Word List

adage
[ad′ ij]
n. a traditional saying; a proverb

circumspection
[sûr′ kəm spek′ shən]
n. watchfulness; caution; care

credibility
[kred′ ə bil′ ə tē]
n. trustworthiness; believability

decipher
[di sī′ fər]
v. to decode; to make out; to make sense of

defraud
[di frôd′]
v. to take away a right, money, or property by deception; to cheat

lax
[laks]
adj. not strict; careless; loose; vague

ordeal
[ôr del′, ôr′ dēl]
n. a harsh or trying test or experience

phishing
[fish′ ing]
n. the practice of luring innocent Internet users to a fake Web site by using real-looking e-mail with the intent to steal personal information or introduce a virus

spam
[spam]
n. junk e-mail; unasked for e-mail, often advertising, sent to multiple individuals
v. 1. to send unwanted e-mail
2. to send to multiple individuals
With a capital "S"
n. a canned meat product made mainly from pork

validity
[və lid′ i tē]
n. 1. authenticity; legal soundness
2. strength; authority

Words to Watch

Which words would you like to practice with a bit more? Pick 3–5 words to study, and list them below. Write the word and its definition, and compose your own sentence using the word correctly. This extra practice could be the final touch to learning a word.

Word	Definition	Your Sentence
1.		
2.		
3.		
4.		
5.		

14

English

Writing Tips

When writing for school, work, or personal use, here are a few points to keep in mind that will make your writing more effective and interesting.

1. Generally Avoid

   The **euphemism**, **cliché**, and **colloquialism** are best avoided in formal writing. Euphemisms are replacement words used for terms that are considered unpleasant. You may have heard a small house called cozy by a real-estate agent or "passed away" used to describe the sad situation of death. You usually want to avoid euphemisms because they tend to hide information or distort a situation.

   Clichés, overused phrases, should be avoided because they can make your writing as dead as a doornail. They are handy in speech because they easily convey an idea: "I'm going to sleep like a log after today's hike." In writing, however, they are usually boring. Make your writing more engaging by creating your own original comparison or plainly state your point: "I'm exhausted."

   Colloquialisms are words or phrases used in everyday speech that usually aren't appropriate in formal writing. For example, "She ain't interested in goin' to the movie with us" uses two colloquialisms: "ain't" for "isn't" and "goin'" for "going." Unless your goal is to capture the flavor of everyday speech, avoid colloquialisms.

2. Use Appropriately

   Introduce an **acronym** properly. If you refer to a CD, your readers may initially be **bewildered** if they are thinking of a compact disc and you mean a certificate of deposit. To use an acronym, first write the full name followed by the acronym in parentheses, British Broadcasting Corporation (BBC). Now you can use the acronym throughout your paper, and the reader will know what you are referring to.

   Watch your use of **homonyms**. Pay attention when you use words that sound alike, and are sometimes spelled alike, but have different meanings, such as which and witch. **Scrutinize** your writing for homonym errors, and if you often mix up certain homonyms, carefully proofread for those.

3. Think Carefully About

   Consider the words you use; you want to be **concise** while still giving enough information to convey your point. During the revision phase, look for wordiness. For example, in "Mary is a loud and noisy woman," *loud* and *noisy* mean the same thing, so only one of the words is needed, and Mary's name indicates she is a woman. The revised "Mary is loud" is more powerful.

   Also learn how much your reader wants you to cover. Does your boss want a **synopsis** of the meeting or a detailed account? You will likely not appreciate the **irony** when you have stayed up all night writing a ten-page report on a sales call to find your boss the next day praising the 200-word summary a colleague wrote in half an hour.

Predicting

For each set, write the definition on the line next to the word to which it belongs. If you are unsure, return to the reading on page 90, and underline any context clues you find. After you've made your predictions, check your answers against the Word List on page 95. Place a checkmark in the box next to each word whose definition you missed. These are the words you'll want to study closely.

Set One

| a commonplace expression | the substitution of a mild expression for one considered harsh |
| a word or abbreviation formed from initial letters | an expression used in informal language | confused |

☐ 1. **euphemism** (line 5) _____

☐ 2. **cliché** (line 5) _____

☐ 3. **colloquialism** (line 5) _____

☐ 4. **acronym** (line 24) _____

☐ 5. **bewildered** (line 24) _____

Set Two

| brief | two or more words that have the same sound but differ in meaning | a summary |
| to examine carefully | a clash between what is expected to happen and what really does |

☐ 6. **homonyms** (line 28) _____

☐ 7. **scrutinize** (line 29) _____

☐ 8. **concise** (line 32) _____

☐ 9. **synopsis** (line 36) _____

☐ 10. **irony** (line 37) _____

Self-Tests

1 Circle the correct word to complete each sentence.

1. When writing you should try to avoid using (clichés, acronyms) because they make your writing as dull as dirt.

2. I gave the judge a (concise, cliché) history of my problems with the store; I thought all the details would bore him.

3. It is important to be aware of (homonyms, euphemisms) because they can be used to mislead people; for example, instead of going to war, a country may be involved in "a military action."

4. Computers have introduced several new (colloquialisms, acronyms) into our language, such as HTML and URL.

5. My cousin always departs using the (euphemism, colloquialism) "outta here."

6. It is important to double-check your writing for (homonym, irony) errors, such as *their, there,* and *they're.*

7. I always (bewilder, scrutinize) my credit card bill each month to make sure I haven't been overcharged.

8. I was able to give my friend a (colloquialism, synopsis) of a five-hundred-page book in two minutes.

9. I was (scrutinized, bewildered) by my son's note that he was going to pick up his dad at the airport. His dad was out front mowing the lawn.

10. The (irony, synopsis) was obvious when my brother said, "Beautiful day for a picnic," as we looked out at the rain soaked street.

2 Match each word below to the appropriate example.

VOCABULARY LIST

acronyms	homonyms	bewilder	synopsis	clichés
concise	euphemisms	irony	scrutinize	colloquialism

1. I see that this hem you just sewed is missing three stitches. _____

2. I thought my friends were planning a surprise party for me; instead, they completely forgot my birthday. _____

3. patience and patients _____

4. I could go for a hamburger for lunch. _____

5. "Tell me about the party." "It was a huge success." _____

6. fit for a king, the greatest thing since sliced bread _____

7. let go, dismissed, made redundant _____

8. ATM, NASA, ASAP, WWW _____

9. The story is about a girl who goes to a house and tries three bowls of porridge. One is too hot, one is too cold, and the other is just right. While she is napping, the bears that live in the house come home and she runs away. _____

10. Why are there golf balls all over the kitchen floor? _____

3 Put a T for true or F for false next to each sentence.

_____ 1. Acronyms are popular with computer users.

_____ 2. "Cool as a cucumber" is a cliché.

_____ 3. Fair (a carnival) and fair (reasonable) are homonyms.

_____ 4. Knowing the best way to get to the museum would show that the person is bewildered.

_____ 5. If it is snowing and your friend says, "It sure is cold," his statement is an example of irony.

_____ 6. "Stocky" and "full-figured" could be considered euphemisms for being overweight.

_____ 7. It is a good idea to use colloquialisms in your college papers.

_____ 8. Talking to your friend for three hours about last night's date would be giving her a concise version.

_____ 9. When your boss looks over your five-page report in two minutes, he has really scrutinized it.

_____10. A synopsis of an article should take less time to read than the original.

Word Wise

Context Clue Mini-Lesson 4

This lesson uses the general meaning of a sentence or passage to help you understand the meaning of the underlined words. In the paragraph below, circle any words that give you clues to the meaning. Then write your own definitions of the underlined words on the lines next to the words that follow the paragraph.

Though I only heard a snippet of my parents' conversation as I walked past their room, it was enough for me to know that I had to leave. They always tried to coddle me, but I was ready to go away to college, and they weren't going to stop me. I would spurn their offer to pay for all of my college expenses if I stayed at home. Though the route to my independence might be tortuous, I was willing to face the challenges to show my parents that I was becoming an adult. I would apply to colleges across the country and look for a job tomorrow.

Your Definition

1. Snippet _____

2. Coddle _____

3. Spurn _____

4. Tortuous _____

Interactive Exercise

Practice using the vocabulary words by completing the following activities.

1. What are two acronyms used on your campus?

   _____

   _____

2. Name something that bewilders you.

   _____

3. List two sets of homonyms you often use. _____

   _____

4. Sometimes clichés contradict each other. What cliché can you think of that is the opposite of "Too many cooks spoil the broth"?

   _____

5. Give an example of a colloquialism you often use. _____

6. Euphemisms are popular for "used" items, such as the term *preowned automobile.* List two other euphemisms for used goods. _____

7. List two things you would want to scrutinize before buying. _____

   _____

8. Write a synopsis of a movie you like. _____

   _____

9. Give an example of a statement you might make to a friend that would show irony. _____

   _____

10. Give a concise recounting of your activities yesterday. _____

   _____

Conversation Starters

An excellent way to review the vocabulary words and help to make them your own is to use them when you are speaking. Gather three to five friends or classmates, and use one or more of the conversation starters below. Before you begin talking, have each person write down six of the vocabulary words he or she will use during the conversation. Share your lists with each other to check that you did not all pick the same six words. Try to cover all of the words you want to study, whether you are reviewing one, two, or more chapters.

1. Did you enjoy being read to as a child? What were some of your favorite books?

2. What are two of your favorite animals? What do you like about these animals? Are they endangered?

3. How careful are you on the computer? What kind of spam do you get?

4. What do you like and dislike about writing?

Word List

acronym
[ak′ rə nim′]

n. a word or abbreviation formed from the initial letters or groups of letters of the words in a name or phrase

bewilder
[bi wil′ dər]

v. to confuse, baffle, or puzzle

cliché
[klē shā′]

n. a commonplace or overused expression or idea

colloquialism
[kə lō′ kwē ə liz′ əm]

n. an expression used in conversational or informal language, not usually appropriate for formal writing

concise
[kən sīs′]

adj. expressing much in a few words; brief

euphemism
[yōō′ fə miz′ əm]

n. the substitution of a mild or vague expression for one considered harsh

homonym
[hom′ ə nim′, hō′ mə-]

n. one of two or more words that have the same sound and sometimes the same spelling but differ in meaning

irony
[ī′ rə nē, ī′ ər-]

n. 1. a clash between what is expected to happen and what really does, often used humorously in literature
2. the use of words to state the opposite of their precise meaning

scrutinize
[skrōōt′ n īz]

v. to examine carefully, especially looking for errors; to inspect

synopsis
[si nop′ sis]

n. a brief statement that gives a general idea; a summary

Words to Watch

Which words would you like to practice with a bit more? Pick 3–5 words to study, and list them below. Write the word and its definition, and compose your own sentence using the word correctly. This extra practice could be the final touch to learning a word.

Word	Definition	Your Sentence
1.		
2.		
3.		
4.		
5.		

15

Word Parts III

Look for words with these **prefixes, roots,** and/or **suffixes** as you work through this book. You may have already seen some of them, and you will see others in later chapters. Learning basic word parts can help you figure out the meanings of unfamiliar words.

prefix: a word part added to the beginning of a word that changes the meaning of the root

root: a word's basic part with its essential meaning

suffix: a word part added to the end of a word; indicates the part of speech

Word Part	Meaning	Examples and Definitions
Prefixes		
am-	love	*amorous:* being in love *amateur:* a person who does something for the love of it without getting paid
eu-	good, well	*euphoria:* a feeling of extreme well-being *eulogy:* a speech that says good things about a person
pan-	all, everywhere	*pandemonium:* disorder everywhere *panorama:* an all-around view
Roots		
-don-, -dot-, -dow-	to give	*donate:* to give away *antidote:* a remedy given to cure something
-fer-	to bring, to carry	*transfer:* to carry across *offer:* to volunteer to bring
-mis-, -mit-	to send	*emissary:* a person sent on a mission *transmit:* to send across
-ven-, -vent-	to come, to move toward	*convene:* to come together *circumvent:* to move around
Suffixes		
-ia (makes a noun)	condition	*hysteria:* a condition of emotional excess *insomnia:* the condition of being unable to sleep
-il, -ile (makes an adjective)	pertaining to or able	*virile:* pertaining to life; strong *versatile:* able to do several different things
-sis (makes a noun)	process or state	*catharsis:* the process of relieving emotional tensions *synopsis:* the process of summarizing

1 Read each definition and choose the appropriate word from the list below. Use each word once. The meaning of the word part is underlined to help you make the connection. Refer to the Word Parts list if you need help.

VOCABULARY LIST

hypothesis	intervene	virile	donor	amorous
eulogy	dismiss	inertia	conference	panorama

1. someone who gives something _____
2. process of making a guess _____
3. a speech on the good qualities of a person, usually given after the person has died _____
4. to come between _____
5. an all-around view _____
6. to send away _____
7. the condition of not moving _____
8. a meeting that brings people together _____
9. pertaining to life _____
10. in a loving mood _____

2 Finish the sentences with the meaning of each word part. Use each meaning once. The word part is underlined to help you make the connection.

VOCABULARY LIST

to give	love	to come	bring	process
condition	sent	all	good	pertaining to

1. The lover _____ a missive the day after the fight asking for forgiveness.
2. My mother uses a hug as a panacea, a cure for _____ problems, and it often works.
3. Milt is going _____ a large endowment to the local art museum because he has always wanted to be a painter.
4. To understand the reading, I had to infer what the author meant, or _____ out his meaning.
5. My boyfriend used the euphemistic phrase "exploring options" to explain why we should break up; he wanted it to sound like a(n) _____ thing.
6. The audience experienced a catharsis during the dramatic end of the play; crying was part of the _____.
7. An amateur plays a sport for the _____ of it.
8. His behavior was juvenile, or _____ being young.
9. Claire's nostalgia for her mother's lasagna was one _____ of her desire to return home.
10. Everyone wants _____ to the event at the stadium, but only people who bought tickets a month ago can get in.

3 Finish the story using the word parts below. Use each word part once. Your knowledge of word parts, as well as the context clues, will help you create the correct words. If you do not understand the meaning of a word you have made, check your dictionary for the definition or to see whether the word exists.

WORD PARTS LIST

am	eu	don	fer	ven	ia	ile	pan	sis	mit

HELPING A FRIEND

I of(1)_____ed to take care of my friend's cat for a week while she went on vacation. She told me he was really (2)_____iable and that I would love spending time with him. I love cats, and I was thinking about getting one myself, so I thought this would be a good opportunity to test my pet skills. I said to drop him by on Friday whenever it was con(3)_____ient for her.

I was surprised when I saw BW. My friend had described him as a frag(4)_____ cat, but he looked hardy to me. She handed me what she referred to as a synop(5)_____ of when he should eat, what he should eat, and how much he should eat. The summary also included how to groom him and what games he liked to play. She said she didn't con(6)_____e his scratching any furniture, so I was supposed to spray him with water if he tried to do so. My (7)_____phoria of having a pet for a week was already disappearing with all her instructions.

After two days, my friend called me terribly upset. I had to talk to her for ten minutes to quiet her hyster(8)_____. Finally, I understood that she had had a dream that my house was filled with (9)_____demonium and that poor BW was upset. I told her everything was calm and that he had just been sitting on my lap while I read. I assured her that we were getting along really well. She insisted that she couldn't relax until I trans(10)_____ted photos showing that BW was all right. I sent her a few photos online and swore it was the last time I'd cat-sit for her.

4 Pick the best definition for each underlined word using your knowledge of word parts. Circle the word part in each of the underlined words.

a. condition of being afraid   f. money or property given by a bride to her husband

b. coming   g. a temple to all gods

c. able to handle easily   h. the process of making a statement

d. a good or painless death   i. to send or happen irregularly

e. to bring on rapidly   j. filled with love

_____ 1. As soon as she saw the puppy, the little girl hugged it and became <u>enamored</u> of it.

_____ 2. <u>Euthanasia</u> is a controversial subject; it can be hard to decide when to end a life.

_____ 3. While in Greece we visited the remains of a <u>pantheon</u> with statues of Athena, Zeus, and other gods.

_____ 4. The <u>advent</u> of the holiday season caused me to sit down and make some plans.

_____ 5. Diana's <u>dowry</u> was considerable: a castle in England and $30,000.

_____ 6. Katy's <u>intermittent</u> letters left us wondering what she was doing in the months she didn't write us.

_____ 7. The offers for starring roles began to <u>proliferate</u> after Karl won an Oscar.

_____ 8. The <u>thesis</u> of my paper is that the college should shorten the semester by two weeks.

_____ 9. I didn't know Colleen had a <u>phobia</u> of flowers until she refused to enter the florist shop.

_____10. After the cat was <u>docile</u>, the doctor was able to operate.

5 A good way to remember word parts is to pick one word that uses a word part and understand how that word part functions in the word. Then you can apply that meaning to other words that have the same word part. Use the following words to help you match the word part to its meaning.

SET ONE

_____ 1. **eu-:** euphoria, euphemism, eulogy   a. love

_____ 2. **-ia:** hysteria, nostalgia, euphoria   b. to give

_____ 3. **am-:** amorous, amiable, amateur   c. condition

_____ 4. **-don-, -dot-, -dow-:** donate, antidote, endow   d. good, well

_____ 5. **-fer-:** transfer, proliferate, fertile   e. to bring, to carry

SET TWO

_____ 6. **-ven-, -vent-:** convene, intervene, circumvent   f. process or state

_____ 7. **-mis-, -mit-:** emissary, transmit, intermittent   g. all, everywhere

_____ 8. **-il, -ile:** virile, docile, fragile   h. to send

_____ 9. **-sis:** synopsis, hypothesis, catharsis   i. to come, to move toward

_____10. **pan-:** pandemonium, panoramic, pantheon   j. pertaining to or able

Interactive Exercise ▨▨▨▨▨▨▨▨▨▨▨▨▨▨▨▨▨▨▨▨▨▨▨▨▨▨▨▨▨▨▨▨▨▨▨▨

Use the dictionary to find a word you don't know that uses each word part listed below. Write the meaning of the word part, the word, and the definition. If your dictionary has the etymology (history) of the word, see how the word part relates to the meaning, and write the etymology after the definition.

Word Part	Meaning	Word	Definition and Etymology

EXAMPLE:

| -ven- | to come, to move toward | venue | the place of an event; literally, a coming toward |

1. *am-* _____

2. *eu-* _____

3. *pan-* _____

4. *-don-* _____

5. *-mis-* _____

Word Wise

A Different Approach: What Should We Call It?

Equipment needed: Unlined and lined paper, pens, and crayons or markers if desired

If you like to draw or are a visual learner, this activity is for you. Gather three other people, and give each one a piece of unlined paper and a piece of lined paper. Each person draws a picture of anything on the unlined paper and signs his or her name at the bottom of the page. Say you are person A. Hand your picture to the person on your left (person B). Person B writes a title for your picture on the lined sheet of paper using one or more of the vocabulary words and puts your name next to the title. Then B passes your drawing to the left; it will now be in the hands of person C. C also writes a title for your picture on his or her lined piece of paper, making sure to write your name next to the title. To practice several words, participants should use different vocabulary words in each title they write. C passes your drawing one more time so person D will have it and give the picture a third title. Because persons B, C, and D have also been passing their drawings to the left, each drawing now has three titles. Hold up one of the pictures, and have each person read aloud the title he or she gave to the picture. As a group, decide which one best fits the picture. Do the same for the other three pictures.

HINT

Marking Words When Reading

When you read for fun, it can be counterproductive to stop and look up every word you don't know—you will become frustrated with reading instead of enjoying it. As this book advocates, looking for context clues is the best way to find the meaning of an unknown word, but sometimes this method doesn't work. There are other ways of keeping track of unfamiliar words; try these methods to see which fits your style.

- Keep a piece of paper and a pen next to you, and write down the word and page number.
- Keep a piece of paper next to you, and rip it into small pieces or use sticky notes. Put a piece between the pages where the word you don't know is located. For added help, write the word on the paper.
- If the book belongs to you, circle the words you don't know and flip through the book later to find them.
- If the book belongs to you, dog-ear the page (turn the corner down) where the word you don't know is located. This method is useful when you don't have paper or a pen handy.
- Repeat the word and page number to yourself a few times. Try to connect the page number to a date to help you remember it.

When you are done reading for the day, get your dictionary and look up the words you marked. The last two methods work best if you don't read many pages before you look up the words or if there are only a few words you don't know. Using these methods will help you learn new words without damaging the fun of reading. Note: If you come across a word you don't know several times and not knowing its meaning hinders your understanding of what is going on, then it's a good idea to stop and look up the word.

Focus on Chapters 11–15

The following activities give you a chance to interact some more with the vocabulary words you've learned. By looking at art, taking tests, answering questions, doing a crossword puzzle, and working with others, you will see which words you know well and which you still need to work with.

Art

Match each picture below to one of the following vocabulary words. Use each word once.

VOCABULARY LIST

omnivorous	encroachment	impede
advocate	spam	homonyms

1. _____

2. _____

3. _____

4. _____

5. _____

6. _____

Self-Tests

1 Pick the word that best completes each sentence.

1. Whenever I hear the _____ "A stitch in time saves nine," I think about the time I didn't fix my leaky sink right away and ended up having to repair my whole bathroom floor.

   a. moratorium   b. homonym   c. adage   d. potential

2. I could appreciate the _____ when my friend said, "I'm going to have lots of fun today: I'm going to the dentist." I knew, like me, he wouldn't really get any enjoyment out of the visit.

   a. advocate   b. irony   c. habitat   d. phishing

3. Gianna was _____ to silly suggestions, so it wasn't surprising when she wore her pajamas to the opera.

   a. concise   b. omnivorous   c. susceptible   d. lax

4. The unusual-looking platypus is _____ to Australia.

   a. lax   b. concise   c. endemic   d. susceptible

5. Fraud is a huge problem on the Internet; users need to be especially aware of Web sites that look real but are really used for _____. Getting personal information to use for dishonest means has become a business for some people.

   a. phishing   b. advocate   c. encroachment   d. irony

2 Pick the vocabulary word that best completes the sentence. Use each word once.

a. bewilders	b. facilitate	c. elicit	d. defraud	e. scrutinizing

1. If your forms and receipts are organized, it will _____ our preparing your tax return.

2. The doctor tried to _____ a response from the patient, but he was too dazed to answer her.

3. My uncle insists on _____ every restaurant bill. He was once charged for food he didn't order, and he doesn't want that to happen again.

4. How anyone can stay at home all day and watch television _____ me. I need to get out and exercise every day.

5. When the boy tried to _____ his neighbor by saying he had mowed her lawn every week, she fired him. She knew he had only been by once that month.

3 Finish the story using the vocabulary words below. Use each word once.

VOCABULARY LIST

acronyms	lax	avert	nurture	ordeal	concise
zoology	potential	innate	habitat	decipher	colloquialisms

IN SOUTH AMERICA

I was excited when my parents announced that we were taking a trip to Chile and Peru. They said they felt I had the (1) _____ to be an archeologist or historian. They wanted to (2) _____ my interests in both areas by exposing me to ancient cultures and historic sites. My usual summer (3) _____ was the couch in front of the television, so this was going to be an exciting adventure. I had been (4) _____ with my Spanish lessons in high school, so I was a bit confused when we got to the airport in Santiago, Chile. I was, however, able to (5) _____ the departure board and find our flight to the Atacama Desert. I had become fascinated with the (6) _____ used to identify airports, so I knew that we were looking for CJC, the airport code for Calama. We had flown from PDX in Portland. We also got help from a woman in the airport. She said to us, "Y'all look like you are lost. Can I help ya?" We guessed from her (7) _____ that she was from the South. She was from Georgia and staying at the same hotel as we were in the desert.

We live on the coast in Oregon, so I was excited to see the desert. Parts of the Atacama Desert have never received recorded rainfall. It is the driest desert in the world. One of our daytrips was to the geysers at El Tatio. To (8) _____ any possible effects of altitude sickness (we would be at 14,000 feet), we ate a light dinner the evening before the trip. The biggest (9) _____ of the whole vacation for me was getting up at 4 a.m. and then trying to catch more sleep on the bumpy ride to the geysers. We arrived at 7 a.m., which our guide said was the best time to see the geysers. On the way back, we saw flamingos, llamas, and a beautiful guanaco. I was especially thrilled to see the guanaco. While I was admiring it, my mother remembered that I had a(n) (10) _____ skill with animals. As a kid, I befriended every dog and cat in our neighborhood. My parents decided to add (11) _____ to the areas I might major in.

I want to keep this account (12) _____, so I will just add that other highlights were seeing the remains of mummified people, visiting the poet Pablo Neruda's house, and exploring the ruins at Machu Picchu. I was right: it was a summer filled with adventure. And my parents were right: the trip did develop in me a desire to study archeology, though I haven't ruled out zoology.

Interactive Exercise ▏▎▍▌▋▊▉▊▋▌▍▎▏▎▍▌▋▊▉▊▋▌▍▎▏▎▍▌▋▊▉▊▋▌▍▎▏▎▍▌▋▊▉

Answer the following questions to further test your understanding of the vocabulary words.

1. What is one thing society should put a moratorium on?

   _____

2. If you were a conservationist (and you may well be), what would you fight hardest to save?

   _____

   _____

3. What can you do to surpass your goals for a course?

   _____

   _____

4. What would a friend have to do to destroy his or her credibility with you?

   _____

5. What is a cliché you especially like to use? Why is that?

   _____

   _____

6. Name two mammals you like. _____

7. When would you want to use circumspection?

   _____

   _____

8. What are two goals you adhere to?

   _____

   _____

9. What are two rules your parents imposed on you as a child?

   _____

   _____

10. Give a synopsis of a book or story you have enjoyed.

   _____

   _____

   _____

11. What would you want to check the validity of before making a decision on whether to buy it or to take action on it?

   _____

12. What are two euphemisms you have used or encountered?

   _____

   _____

Crossword Puzzle

Use the following words to complete the crossword puzzle. Use each word once.

VOCABULARY LIST

acronym

adage

advocate

bewilder

circumspection

colloquialism

decipher

elicit

encroachment

endemic

facilitate

habitat

homonyms

impede

innate

irony

omnivorous

ordeal

spam

susceptible

Across

2. open to an influence
4. a harsh test or experience
6. a person who supports a cause
7. eating all types of food
9. for dolphins, the ocean
14. You can't come in here.
15. watchfulness
18. to make easier
19. to make sense of
20. to draw or bring out

Down

1. to confuse or puzzle
3. They ain't got nothin' I want.
5. The early bird catches the worm.
8. junk e-mail
10. the use of words to state the opposite of their precise meaning
11. an intrusion
12. RSVP or NBA
13. to, too, two
16. natural to a particular area
17. possessed at birth

Mix It Up

Category Race

Get together with a dozen classmates or so and form three to four teams. Each team needs a set of flash cards for the words to be studied and a blank sheet of paper. Each team thinks of a category, writes it on the top of the sheet of paper, and places flash cards that fit in that category underneath the heading. Alternatively, you can write the words on the paper. After ten minutes, call time. Each group reads its category and words. There may be some disagreement on whether a word fits the category; discuss the word and its meanings to decide these issues. The team that supplies the most words wins. Another way to play is to give each team the same category and seven minutes to record its words. You can also do this activity with each person making his or her own category list. If you do it individually, you can compete with just three or four people.

Possible categories:

1. travel words
2. words that show trouble
3. health-related words
4. history words
5. love-life words
6. crime-related words
7. business-related words
8. undesirable qualities

Sample sheet:

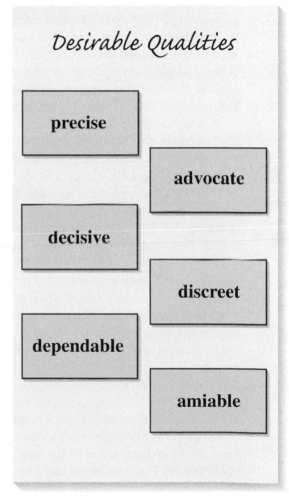

Life in Medieval Europe

The fall of the Roman Empire in the fifth century A.D. marked the beginning of **medieval** times, also known as the Middle Ages or the Dark Ages. Life in western Europe became
5 dangerous and chaotic. Tribes of **barbarians** invaded—the Magyars from the east and Vikings from the north—killing and **plundering** as they rode. Because safety became the primary concern, a new way of
10 life called **feudalism** developed. Under this system, people lived together for protection on a parcel of land called a *manor*. Every manor had a castle, a village, and a Catholic church.

During the Middle Ages, kings were said to have the "divine right" given by God to rule. However,
15 they could not govern effectively since their landholdings were large and communication was slow and difficult. For this reason, kings formed political **alliances** with lesser nobility. The nobles were entrusted to govern part of the king's lands. The lord of a manor had absolute authority over the peasants, who were called *serfs*. Most serfs were bound to the land and treated as slaves. In a special ceremony held each year, the peasants had to **proclaim** their loyalty to the lord of the manor. They paid **homage** to the lord by
20 declaring that they would work his land, pay taxes, and provide troops to fight when necessary. The lord would affirm that hc would do his duty to protect the serfs during times of danger.

Another powerful group was the clergy. Monks living in monasteries were among the few who were educated; they kept historical records and translated texts. Priests and bishops were much worldlier. They were often involved in politics and other **secular** activities. The feudal system gave
25 the nobility and the clergy wealth and power, while the other ninety percent of the people labored their entire lives in extreme poverty.

Women also didn't enjoy many **privileges**. Noble women usually had two options: marry or enter a nunnery. If a woman married, it was usually by the time she was fourteen. Noble women supervised household matters. Peasant women were responsible for running the house and helping with the farming.
30 Women usually did the weaving and took care of the dairy. A noble woman might get some education at home, and nunneries offered a few schools, but for the most part women were uneducated.

In 1347, a ship returning from the East arrived in Sicily filled with sick sailors. The townspeople were scared and refused to let the ship stay in port; however, some of the rats on the ship had already come ashore. The fleas on the rats carried the **plague**, and it spread through Sicily. It was a fast-acting
35 disease with most people killed within a week of the first signs—black blotches on the skin, a black tongue, swelling under the armpits, chills. The disease spread to Italy and on through the rest of Europe. By 1350 the disease appeared to be gone, but it was to resurface for short periods for the next 300 years. By 1400 approximately one-third of Europe's population, about 50 million people, were dead. Many peasants died, and, with a smaller labor force, they became more important. The serfs started to demand
40 fairer treatment, and by the time the plague disappeared forever, feudalism was also dead.

Predicting

For each set, write the definition on the line next to the word to which it belongs. If you are unsure, return to the reading on page 108, and underline any context clues you find. After you've made your predictions, check your answers against the Word List on page 113. Place a checkmark in the box next to each word whose definition you missed. These are the words you'll want to study closely.

Set One

agreements to cooperate	of the Middle Ages	a political system based on holding land	savages	robbing

❑ 1. **medieval** (line 3) _____

❑ 2. **barbarians** (line 6) _____

❑ 3. **plundering** (line 8) _____

❑ 4. **feudalism** (line 10) _____

❑ 5. **alliances** (line 16) _____

Set Two

worldly	honor	advantages	a widespread disease	to state publicly

❑ 6. **proclaim** (line 19) _____

❑ 7. **homage** (line 19) _____

❑ 8. **secular** (line 24) _____

❑ 9. **privileges** (line 27) _____

❑ 10. **plague** (line 34) _____

Self-Tests

1 Circle the correct word to complete each sentence.

1. For most people, the (secular, medieval) period was filled with hardships.

2. The movie was a(n) (homage, alliance) to the great director Alfred Hitchcock.

3. It was considered a (privilege, barbarian) to host the city's annual awards banquet.

4. The museum was (proclaimed, plundered) during the riots, and several valuable paintings were lost forever.

5. The (secular, medieval) life does not appeal to some people, so they choose to live more spiritually.

6. It is unlikely that (alliance, feudalism) will return as a dominant political system soon.

7. Four of the survivors made a(n) (privilege, alliance), which forced the other two to manage on their own.

8. Carlos acts like a (barbarian, feudalism) when he tears into a crab dinner.

9. When Sumiko (proclaimed, plagued) her intention to try out for the swim team, she got her whole family's support.

10. Aches and pains have (plagued, plundered) Gwen since she slipped on the ice last week.

2 Finish the story with the best word for each blank. Use each word once.

Sir Geoffrey impatiently waited for his squire Thaddeus to finish preparing his suit of armor for battle. Matters were frenzied in the castle. News had come that an especially fierce

(1) _____ tribe had been killing and

(2) _____ its way through neighboring kingdoms and was headed this way. Loyal to Lord Richard, Geoffrey would serve whenever he was needed. In Geoffrey's hand was a letter he had hastily prepared for the object of his affection, Lady Sarah. Sir Geoffrey felt that, after two years of courtship, it was fitting to (3) _____ his love before he left for combat. He also felt that it was his

(4) _____ to make a special request of Lady Sarah. Besides the usual poetry and pledges of love, he asked her to pay (5) _____ to his memory should he die in battle.

While Sir Geoffrey prepared for battle, a very different scene was taking place in another part of the kingdom. Brother Joseph knew he was keeping history alive. He had no regrets about being a monk. He was one of the few who could read and write, so he was able to keep records of the past and present. The (6) _____ world outside the church with its temptations had never attracted him. He hadn't wanted to be a priest, either. He preferred the quiet walls of the monastery during these uncertain (7) _____ times. He wondered what this period of history would be remembered for. For everyone outside the monastery, the way of life was (8) _____. Kings gave pieces of land to nobles, and the nobles gave land to others. This system was an excellent way to make powerful <u>(9)</u>   . The agreements helped both sides, but there were also many wars. He had also heard reports of a great <u>(10)</u>   sweeping through Europe. He wondered if the death and destruction would reach his quiet monastery. He hoped not. But the outside world was not his business. It was time for Brother Joseph to return to his writing.

3 For each set, write the letter of the most logical analogy. See Completing Analogies on page 6 for instructions and practice.

Set One

_____ 1. plague : please ::

_____ 2. pilot : flies ::

_____ 3. late 1900s : condominium ::

_____ 4. barbarian : savage ::

_____ 5. secular : office ::

a. king : proclaims

b. religious : church

c. considerate : kind

d. depressed : overjoyed

e. medieval : castle

Set Two

_____ 6. read : writer ::

_____ 7. feudalism : Middle Ages ::

_____ 8. excellent : awful ::

_____ 9. leaves : rake ::

_____ 10. alliance : cooperate ::

f. silver : plunder

g. play : perform

h. homage : king

i. hippies : 1960s

j. privilege : misfortune

Word Wise

Collocations

The city council agreed to fund a mural that would *pay homage to* the town's pioneers and their hard work in building the community. (Chapter 17)

Word Pairs

Secular/Religious: Secular (Chapter 17) means "worldly; not holy or religious," while religious means "spiritual; holy." Secular matters were taken care of by the businessmen, while the clergy handled the religious needs of the community.

Interesting Etymologies

Homage (Chapter 17): comes from a medieval ceremony called *homage*, from the French word *homme*, or "man." In the ceremony, a serf had to pledge his allegiance to his lord by stating that he would be his "man." The serf also accepted the terms of his working the lord's land, and the lord on his part had to agree to protect the serf in times of danger. Today homage means "honor or tribute," but it does not need to be mutual. A director can make a film in homage to another director's style, but that director does not need to respond in any way.

Interactive Exercise |||||||||||||||||||||||||||||||||||||||||||||||||||||||||||||||||||||

Make associations between the vocabulary word and other words or situations. Give two examples for each word.

EXAMPLES:

plunder   _money_   medieval   _castles_

            Vikings   _knights_

1. barbarian   _____   _____
2. feudalism   _____   _____
3. proclaim   _____   _____
4. secular   _____   _____
5. alliance   _____   _____
6. plague   _____   _____
7. homage   _____   _____
8. medieval   _____   _____
9. privilege   _____   _____
10. plunder   _____   _____

Word Part Reminder

Below are a few short exercises to help you review the word parts you have been learning. Fill in the missing word part from the list, and circle the meaning of the word part found in each sentence. Try to complete the questions without returning to the Word Parts chapter, but if you get stuck, look back at Chapter 15.

            am   don   mit   ia

1. I need to send a message to my sister across the country. I think the fastest way to trans_____ my news is to write her an e-mail.

2. I hope Tom is willing to give me a break. If he can par_____ my bad mood last night, I promise I will be a better house guest.

3. I am in love with my new car. I am so en_____ored of it that I slept in it last night.

4. Luckily my husband's condition isn't serious. He usually only experiences insomn_____ when he is really stressed at work.

Word List

alliance
[ə lī′ əns]
   n. an agreement to cooperate; an association

barbarian
[bär bâr′ ē ən]
   n. 1. a savage; a brute
      2. a person without culture

feudalism
[fyo͞od′ l iz′ əm]
   n. a political system of the Middle Ages, based on holding land

homage
[hom′ ij, om′-]
   n. honor; tribute

medieval
[med′ ē vəl, mid ē′ vəl]
   adj. of the Middle Ages

plague
[plāg]
   n. 1. a widespread disease; an outbreak
      2. any widespread evil; any annoyance
   v. to trouble; to annoy; to make miserable

plunder
[plun′ dər]
   v. to rob by force, as in war; to raid

privilege
[priv′ ə lij, priv′ lij]
   n. an advantage; a right

proclaim
[prō klām′, prə-]
   v. 1. to state publicly
      2. to praise publicly
      3. to prohibit publicly

secular
[sek′ yə lər]
   adj. worldly; not holy or religious

Words to Watch

Which words would you like to practice with a bit more? Pick 3–5 words to study, and list them below. Write the word and its definition, and compose your own sentence using the word correctly. This extra practice could be the final touch to learning a word.

	Word	Definition	Your Sentence
1.			
2.			
3.			
4.			
5.			

18

Art History

Florence Beckons

GUIDE: Welcome to day four of our art history tour of Italy. I hope you are all refreshed after our arrival last night from Rome. It is said that Florence is the birthplace of the **Renaissance**. The city is a living museum **endowed** with numerous examples of the rebirth of art and architecture. Renaissance style is based on two elements: a renewed interest in the classical artistic forms of the ancient Greeks
5   and Romans and an interest in **humanism**, the importance of the individual. This morning we are go-
ing to visit the world-famous Duomo, the cathedral with the octagonal dome that has become the recognizable symbol of
10 Florence and, really, of all the region of Tuscany. As we walk through Florence, consider how lucky we are that so many people had the **foresight** to main-
15 tain and care for the buildings and artwork we will be seeing. Later in the day we will visit the Palazzo Vecchio and the Uffizi Gallery.
20   Ladies and gentlemen, here is the Duomo, which is also called *Santa Maria del Fiore* (St. Mary of the Flower). It is the result of the **fertile** imagina-
25 tions of artists and architects from the thirteenth to the nine-teenth centuries. The original

The magnificent Duomo, Santa Maria del Fiore, *dominates the Florence skyline.*

design for the cathedral was created by Arnulfo di Cambio at the end of the thirteenth century and completed in the fourteenth century. The interior of the Duomo includes not only the dominant gothic
30 style of pre-Renaissance times but classical elements as well. The **cupola** was the product of the brilliant Renaissance architect Filippo Brunelleschi in the fifteenth century. The dome has been an inspiration for the Capitol in Washington, D.C., and St. Paul's Cathedral in London. Finally, the **façade** that you see before you was completed in 1875. Not only did the cathedral go through **intermittent** structural changes during this long period, but it was also **adorned** inside and out with paintings and
35 sculptures. Of particular beauty are the **frescoes** painted directly on the interior walls of the cathedral. Please follow me inside.

Predicting

For each set, write the definition on the line next to the word to which it belongs. If you are unsure, return to the reading on page 114, and underline any context clues you find. After you've made your predictions, check your answers against the Word List on page 119. Place a checkmark in the box next to each word whose definition you missed. These are the words you'll want to study closely.

Set One

concern for the future	period of European history	very productive	furnished

philosophy emphasizing the importance of human interests and values

❑ 1. **Renaissance** (line 2) _____

❑ 2. **endowed** (line 3) _____

❑ 3. **humanism** (line 5) _____

❑ 4. **foresight** (line 14) _____

❑ 5. **fertile** (line 24) _____

Set Two

dome	irregular	paintings done on moist plaster	decorated	exterior of a building

❑ 6. **cupola** (line 30) _____

❑ 7. **façade** (line 32) _____

❑ 8. **intermittent** (line 33) _____

❑ 9. **adorned** (line 34) _____

❑ 10. **frescoes** (line 35) _____

Self-Tests ▥▥▥

1 Match each term with its synonym in Set One and its antonym in Set Two.

SYNONYMS

SET ONE

_____ 1. adorn   a. dome

_____ 2. endow   b. painting

_____ 3. fresco   c. give

_____ 4. intermittent   d. decorate

_____ 5. cupola   e. irregular

ANTONYMS

_____ 6. façade   f. carelessness

_____ 7. fertile   g. real

_____ 8. foresight   h. stagnation

_____ 9. humanism   i. barren

_____ 10. renaissance   j. divinity

2 Complete the sentences using the vocabulary words. Use each word once.

VOCABULARY LIST

fertile	fresco	endow	adorn	humanism
cupola	façade	foresight	Renaissance	intermittent

1. The _____ of the new hotel is quite grand. I can't wait to see the inside.

2. The day was supposed to be filled with _____ showers, so we cancelled the picnic.

3. Senator Mills has promised to _____ a million dollars to the college when he dies.

4. The settlers decided to stop in the valley when they saw how _____ the soil was.

5. I'm glad I had the _____ to bring a piece of fruit. I am starving, and the doctor is an hour behind in his appointments.

6. The _____ on the capitol building is huge. We could see it from a hill five miles from town.

7. To make the area more attractive, the planning committee has decided to _____ the area with fountains and public artwork.

8. On my trip to Italy last summer, I was especially impressed with a(n) _____ of a garden scene. Despite some peeling paint, the flowers still looked so real.

9. If I could travel back in time, I would like to visit the _____ to see the great achievements in art and architecture actually being created.

10. Next term I am going to pursue a semester of _____ by taking courses in literature, philosophy, and art.

3 Finish the readings with the best word for each blank. Use each word once.

VOCABULARY LIST

humanism	endowed	Renaissance	fertile	frescoes
intermittent	adorned	cupola	foresight	façades

THE PAST

The (1) _____ took place in Europe roughly from the fourteenth to the seventeenth centuries.

A great revival of interest in art, literature, science, and other areas of learning occurred that had not

been felt since the height of the ancient Greek and Roman civilizations. There was greater belief in the abilities of humankind; this new attitude toward the individual was known as (2)_____, and it led to education for more people. One of the most (3)_____ minds of the period belonged to Leonardo da Vinci. He was a sculptor, painter, inventor, philosopher, and writer. Among the most famous (4)_____ of all time are those Michelangelo painted on the ceiling of the Sistine Chapel in Rome. The world was also (5)_____ with new discoveries such as the revelation from Copernicus that the center of the universe is the sun and not the Earth, as was previously thought.

THE PRESENT

American society has taken a(n) (6)_____ interest in the architectural styles of the past. Greek columns decorate the (7)_____ of banks and buildings on many college campuses, and Victorian gingerbread houses dominate some neighborhoods. American architecture is interesting because buildings can be (8)_____ with sculptures and paintings representing people and achievements from anywhere and any time. Looking at the (9)_____ that usually sits atop a state capitol building, one can feel proud that the architectural styles from the past are still used and also know that innovations are part of modern architecture as evidenced by the high-rises found in most cities. It can only be hoped that people have the (10)_____ to remember the value of past contributions when designing buildings for the future.

Word Wise

Context Clue Mini-Lesson 5

This lesson combines the techniques you have practiced in the four previous lessons. You will be looking for synonyms, antonyms, examples, and general meaning to help you understand the underlined words. In the paragraph below, circle any clues you find and then write the types of clues and your definitions on the lines next to the words that follow the paragraph.

The company can no longer tolerate your recent unscrupulous behavior. We have discovered that you have been stealing company supplies, taking three-hour lunches, and viewing inappropriate material on the Internet on company time. Because of your long association with the firm, we are giving you the opportunity to leave of your own volition. If you do not resign by Tuesday, you will be fired by the end of the week. We do not want to create unnecessary acrimony between you and the company. To maintain some harmony in our relationship, we will be having a small going-away party for you on Thursday. I'm sorry these last few months have had to mar an otherwise positive working relationship, but the damage has been done, and it is time for you to leave.

Type of Context Clue and Your Definition

1. Unscrupulous _____

2. Volition _____

3. Acrimony _____

4. Mar _____

Interactive Exercise |||||||||||||||||||||||||||||||||||||||||||||||||||||||||||||||||||||

Answer the following questions.

1. What are three skills you are endowed with?

   _____

   _____

   _____

2. Do you like buildings that have a cupola? Explain why or why not. _____

   _____

3. What is one characteristic of the Renaissance? _____

4. What would you paint a fresco of? _____

5. What objects adorn your bedroom? _____

6. What are two architectural elements that you might find on the façade of a building (for example, statues)?

   _____   _____

7. What is something society should have foresight about? _____

8. What two activities have you done intermittently?

   _____

   _____

9. Humanism is also the study of the humanities; what area in the humanities are you most interested in?

   _____

10. To have a fertile day, what are two things you need to do?

   _____

   _____

HINT

Test-Taking Technique

If you get stuck on one question when doing a matching test, go on to the next one. When you finish answering the questions that are easy for you, see which questions and choices are left. With fewer choices the answers should be easier to find. For an example of where you can use this technique, look back at Self-Test 1 in this chapter.

Word List

adorn
[ə dôrn′]
v. to decorate; to beautify

cupola
[kyo͞o′ pə lə]
n. a dome or domelike structure

endow
[en dou′]
v. 1. to furnish; to equip
2. to give money as a donation

façade
[fə säd′]
n. 1. exterior of a building, especially the front, and usually impressive
2. a false appearance

fertile
[fûr′ tl]
adj. 1. very productive
2. capable of having children

foresight
[fôr′ sīt′]
n. 1. concern for the future; carefulness
2. knowledge of the future

fresco
[fres′ kō]
n. painting done on moist plaster

humanism
[hyo͞o′ mə niz′ əm]
n. 1. philosophy emphasizing the importance of human interests and values, dating from the time of the Renaissance
2. study of the humanities (literature, languages, philosophy, art)

intermittent
[in′ tər mit′ nt]
adj. stopping and beginning again; periodic; irregular

Renaissance
[ren′ i säns′, -zäns′]
n. 1. a period of European history from the fourteenth to the seventeenth centuries in which there was renewed interest in learning and discovery
2. (small r) a rebirth; a revival

Words to Watch

Which words would you like to practice with a bit more? Pick 3–5 words to study, and list them below. Write the word and its definition, and compose your own sentence using the word correctly. This extra practice could be the final touch to learning a word.

Word	Definition	Your Sentence
1.		
2.		
3.		
4.		
5.		

Political Science

Politics Overseas

June 23

I am so glad I signed up for this summer program! Visiting different countries to learn about their political systems is proving to be one of the most exciting things I have ever done. It is our third day in England, and today we learned more about the constitutionalmonarchy system and Britain's royalty. I hadn't realized that the
5 king or queen is a **figurehead** who doesn't have any real power. The monarchy has been losing power since 1215 when King John was forced by the nobels to sign the Magna Carta, which guarenteed more rights to the people. Still, if a king or queen has enough **charisma**, he or she can have an influence on the country. Queen Elizabeth II seems to be popular with most of the people I've
10 met. Queen Victoria was also admired by the people. The British Empire reached its **zenith** during her reign from 1837 to 1901. She ruled for 64 years, the longest of any monarch. She really strengthened Britain's power by marrying her nine children to various royal families in Europe, including those in Denmark, Russia, and Germany. During her reign, the British **realm** covered almost one quarter
15 of the planet. Britain ruled over India, Canada, Australia, Hong Kong, several areas in Africa, some Caribbean islands, and other small islands such as Fiji. The saying "The sun never sets on the British Empire" was definitely true during her reign.

July 15

We have been in Africa for almost two weeks, and it has been enlightening. I am
20 happy to note that there are several efforts to fix the problems the continent has been facing. The cacao farms we visited in Ghana are now dealing with fair trade organizations that pay the people enough so that they can earn a reasonable living. The preserves we traveled through in Rwanda are employing local people as conservationists and working to protect endangered animals like the mountain gorilla. And we witnessed the success of Nobel prize winner
25 Wangari Maathai's tree-planting campaign to reforest Kenya. Still, there are problems of AIDS, poverty, and corrupt governments hat leave people at risk for famine and disease, especially from unsafe drinking water. Yesterday we attended a political rally in an unstable country before the **impending** election on Friday. With only three days before the election, the current **regime** seems worried. A plot to **depose** the corrupt president failed last year,
30 and now a new party has formed that represents the poor, which seems to be a lot of the country. As we drove around, I saw that the country's **infrastructure**—roads, bridges, pipelines—is falling apart. And from what I've heard in the streets, the government doesn't care. We are leaving on Thursday because problems are expected if the president wins reelection. I hear that he is bribing people to vote for him and that the votes won't be counted
35 by an impartial group. If he does win, rumors are that a **coup** may be staged by the opposition. It will be hard to **wrest** control of the country from the president, but the people might be angry enough to do it. It would be exciting to stay and see what happens, but I understand the college's concern for our safety.

Predicting

For each set, write the definition on the line next to the word to which it belongs. If you are unsure, return to the reading on page 120, and underline any context clues you find. After you've made your predictions, check your answers against the Word List on page 125. Place a checkmark in the box next to each word whose definition you missed. These are the words you'll want to study closely.

Set One

> charm   a person in a position of leadership who has no real power   about to happen   an empire
>
> the highest point

❑   1. **figurehead** (line 6) _____

❑   2. **charisma** (line 9) _____

❑   3. **zenith** (line 12) _____

❑   4. **realm** (line 15) _____

❑   5. **impending** (line 30) _____

Set Two

> foundations countries depend on   to remove from an important position   government
>
> to take through force   overthrow of the government

❑   6. **regime** (line 31) _____

❑   7. **depose** (line 31) _____

❑   8. **infrastructure** (line 33) _____

❑   9. **coup** (line 36) _____

❑ 10. **wrest** (line 37) _____

Self-Tests

1 Put a T for true or F for false next to each sentence.

_____ 1. The Orpilla family has an impending vacation—the couple plan to travel to Europe when they retire in twenty years.

_____ 2. A king who makes sure his people are well fed and educated is one the public would want to depose.

_____ 3. A person usually reaches the zenith of his or her career the second day on a job.

_____ 4. An interest in the stars could lead someone into the realm of astronomy.

_____ 5. You can often wrest the meaning of a story if you think about it for a while.

_____ 6. Most notable leaders possess charisma (e.g. Franklin D. Roosevelt, Gandhi, Cleopatra).

_____ 7. There have been three coups in the last ten years in the United States.

_____ 8. A regime that doesn't care if most of its people are poor would be called kind.

_____ 9. Being a figurehead would likely frustrate an honest and motivated person.

_____ 10. To make sure a city's infrastructure does not fall apart, it should be checked regularly.

2 Match each vocabulary word with its synonym in Set One and its antonym in Set Two.

SYNONYMS

SET ONE

_____ 1. territory   a. charisma

_____ 2. allure   b. infrastructure

_____ 3. misrepresent   c. regime

_____ 4. government   d. wrest

_____ 5. foundation   e. realm

ANTONYMS

SET TWO

_____ 6. install   f. impending

_____ 7. peace   g. figurehead

_____ 8. lowest   h. coup

_____ 9. distant   i. zenith

_____10. organizer   j. depose

3 Fill in each blank with the appropriate vocabulary word. Use each word once.

VOCABULARY LIST				
regime	infrastructure	charisma	realm	zenith
depose	wrest	figurehead	impending	coup d'etat

1. The board decided it was time to _____ the president of the company. He had begun acting like a king and not part of a team.

2. In the _____ of sports, Venus Williams, Hank Aaron, Michelle Kwan, and Lance Armstrong are considered among the greats.

3. My _____ biology midterm is making me nervous. I haven't opened the textbook all semester.

4. The small African nation is being governed by a military _____.

5. The voters have approved a tax to improve the water plant, bridges, streets, and other parts of the _____ of their city.

6. Despite the financial scandal, the mayor was elected to another term because of his
   _____.

7. The children tried to _____ control of the company from their father when they felt
   his mental health was failing.

8. Although Gavin was a union representative, he was just a(n) _____. He had no real
   power.

9. The government changed hands overnight in a sudden political _____.

10. The actor felt he had reached the _____ of his career after he won an Academy Award.

Word Wise

Collocations

The child had a *fertile imagination;* she told her mother that she
had turned her bed into a sailing ship. (Chapter 18)

The *charismatic leader* persuaded the people to revolt against
the *military regime* and start a democracy. (Chapter 19)

It is within the *realm of possibility* to fix our city's *crumbling
infrastructure* if our taxes are used wisely. Our roads, pipes, and
bridges have not been properly maintained for years. (Chapter 19)

Word Pairs

Foresight/Hindsight: Foresight (Chapter 18) means "knowledge
of the future," and hindsight means "awareness after the fact."
Norma's foresight helped us avoid sitting in traffic; she knew which routes were the most crowded on
Fridays. In hindsight, we should have brought warmer clothes on the trip; it was still cold in the
mountains in April.

Zenith/Nadir: Zenith (Chapter 19) means "the highest point," while nadir means "the lowest point."
Helen felt she had reached the zenith of her professional life when she was awarded a Nobel Prize. It
was a far cry from the nadir when she was an alcoholic living on the streets.

Connotations and Denotations

Charisma (Chapter 19): denotation—"special quality of leadership that inspires devotion." Who do
you picture as a charismatic leader? People often see the word as applying to leaders such as
Gandhi, Franklin Delano Roosevelt, and Joan of Arc (normally considered good people fighting for
worthy causes). When someone is said to have charisma, it is generally considered a positive trait;
however, the word can equally apply to Adolph Hitler, who is usually not highly regarded as a
person. Yet Hitler had the ability to inspire the devotion of thousands of people, which fits the
denotation of charisma.

Interesting Etymologies

Figurehead (Chapter 19): comes from the ornamental figureheads found on the front of sailing
ships. These decorative figures (often of women's heads or upper bodies) did not serve any purpose
in the operation of the ship, leading to the definition of figurehead as "a person in a position of
leadership who has no real power."

Interactive Exercise

Pretend you have signed up for the program to study different political systems. Write a letter home telling about something you have learned or seen in one of the places on your trip. You may choose to use the United States on a visit to Washington, D.C., or one of the state capitals, or pick a country with which you are familiar. Use at least six of the vocabulary words.

Dear _____,

_____

_____

_____

_____

_____

_____

_____

_____

_____

_____

_____

_____

_____

So long, _____

HINT

Study Often

Don't try to fit all of your studying into one session before a test. Look at your notes for a class often. Review them the day you write them while the information is fresh in your mind in case you want to add material. Do a weekly review so that, as you learn new material, you can build on the old information. These same ideas apply to learning vocabulary. Look often at the flash cards you make. Even taking ten minutes a day to study the words for that week will help you remember the meanings. While you are waiting for another class to start, for a friend who is late, or for the bus to come, take some of that time to review the words.

Word List

charisma
[kə riz′ mə]
n. a special quality of leadership that inspires devotion; charm; allure

coup or **coup d'etat**
[kōō] [kōō′ dā tä′]
n. overthrow of the government; revolt

depose
[di pōz′]
v. to remove from an important position or office; to dethrone

figurehead
[fig′ yər hed′]
n. a person in a position of leadership who has no real power

impending
[Im pen′ding]
adj. 1. about to happen; in the near future; approaching
2. threatening; looming

infrastructure
[in′ frə struk′ chər]
n. 1. foundations countries depend on, such as roads and power plants
2. the basic features of an organization

realm
[relm]
n. 1. a territory ruled by a king or queen; an empire
2. an area of interest, knowledge, or activity

regime
[ri zhēm′, rā-]
n. government; period of time that a person or political system is in power

wrest
[rest]
v. 1. to extract or take through force or continuous effort
2. to misrepresent or twist the meaning or use of

zenith
[zē′ nith]
n. the highest point; the peak; the top

Words to Watch

Which words would you like to practice with a bit more? Pick 3–5 words to study, and list them below. Write the word and its definition, and compose your own sentence using the word correctly. This extra practice could be the final touch to learning a word.

	Word	Definition	Your Sentence
1.			
2.			
3.			
4.			
5.			

20

Business

Making It on Your Own

Succeeding in Business

Do you have what it takes to be an **entrepreneur**? Do you have an idea for a product people must have? Do you have a skill you have wanted to turn into a business? Starting your own business **venture** can be hard work but also extremely rewarding. The Business Department is starting a series of classes on how to run a successful business. Whatever you specialize in doing—baking, writing, working with computers—can now make you money. Those who are brave enough to face the problems of running a business will also find the rewards of being one's own boss.

The following are some of the most **prominent** traits found amongst entrepreneurs. Do you have a **propensity** for any of these important traits?

Passion. A major **asset** to starting your own business is being excited about your product or service. If you don't love it, how do you expect other people to? You need to be willing to proclaim your resume service the best there is, your jewelry creations the most beautiful, or your dog-training skills the greatest.

Determination. The biggest **liability** a business owner can have is a lack of drive. You have to find the way to succeed when things aren't going your way. On the first day Debbie Fields opened her cookie store, no one had come in by noon. She didn't give up! She put a batch of her cookies on a tray and walked outside to distribute them to people walking by. People loved them and followed her back to the store. From there the Mrs. Fields cookie empire grew.

Flexibility. When running a business, you will need to **modify** your plans as everything will not always go your way. Even finding your **niche** in a business calls for flexible thinking. Reed Hastings was upset when he returned his videos to a store and was told he owed $40 in late fees. Angry about the fees, Hastings decided there should be a better system. The idea for Netflix was born. Hastings found a special place in the crowded world of video rentals because he saw a need that others were not meeting. Hastings used his degree in computer science to create a system that allows people to rent videos for a flat monthly fee with no late charges using their computers.

Humor. If you are a **jovial** person, you can cope with the stress of running a business. If you always get angry or upset, your problems are only going to **proliferate**. If you can keep your sense of humor, your problems will not grow to unmanageable proportions. You will be working with people who are your employees or clients, and they will want to deal with a friendly and cheerful person.

If these traits fit you, sign up for the courses in the Succeeding in Business program. Among other skills, learn important business terminology, how to create a marketing plan, and ways to deal with legal issues.
Call (326) 555-3579 today to get a catalogue of the course offerings.

Predicting

For each set, write the definition on the line next to the word to which it belongs. If you are unsure, return to the reading on page 126, and underline any context clues you find. After you've made your predictions, check your answers against the Word List on page 131. Place a checkmark in the box next to each word whose definition you missed. These are the words you'll want to study closely.

Set One

| a leaning | a business enterprise | a desirable thing | leading | one who assumes the risks of a business |

❑ 1. **entrepreneur** (line 1) _____

❑ 2. **venture** (line 3) _____

❑ 3. **prominent** (line 8) _____

❑ 4. **propensity** (line 9) _____

❑ 5. **asset** (line 10) _____

Set Two

| to change the form of | to grow | cheerful | an appropriate place | a disadvantage |

❑ 6. **liability** (line 15) _____

❑ 7. **modify** (line 23) _____

❑ 8. **niche** (line 24) _____

❑ 9. **jovial** (line 31) _____

❑ 10. **proliferate** (line 32) _____

Self-Tests

1 Circle the correct meaning of each vocabulary word.

1. asset:	a worthless thing	a desirable thing
2. jovial:	cheerful	sad
3. niche:	a lobby	a recess
4. proliferate:	to decrease	to increase
5. propensity:	a preference	indifference
6. venture:	to fear	to brave
7. entrepreneur:	one who assumes the risks of a business	one who works for others
8. prominent:	unimportant	notable

9. liability: a disadvantage   an advantage

10. modify: vary   steady

2 Use the vocabulary words to finish the students' statements about why they are taking classes in the Succeeding in Business program.

Set One

VOCABULARY LIST

propensity	entrepreneur	venture	niche	modify

I have enrolled in this program because my family has a(n)

(1) _____ for baking. My grandfather owned a donut shop,

and my mother won the county fair pie-baking contest for eight years

straight. Now I want to (2) _____ into baking for a profit. I

think I have discovered my (3) _____ in the business: cook-

ies for every holiday. I have recipes and designs for cookies from

Arbor Day to Valentine's Day. I can even (4) _____ my

cookies for a client's special occasion. Whatever they want, I can

make. I have a passion for cooking, so I am sure I will be a good

(5) _____. I can't wait to start my catering business.

Set Two

VOCABULARY LIST

asset	liability	jovial	prominent	proliferate

I am a(n) (6) _____ person. I get along well with

others, and animals love me. I want to start a pet-sitting

business. My greatest (7) _____ is my flexibility.

I can take on a job at a moment's notice. I want to learn

how to make flyers that will catch a person's attention and

find out the (8) _____ locations around town to

distribute them so I can get the most exposure. I am

hoping my clients will (9) _____, and then I can

hire my brother. He is also great with animals. The only (10) _____ I can see is that sometimes

I get too attached to an animal I sit for and I don't want to leave, but I can work on that problem.

3 For each set, complete the analogies. See Completing Analogies on page 6 for instructions and practice.

Set One

VOCABULARY LIST

entrepreneur	modify	liability	niche	venture

1. surfboard : water :: vase : _____
2. embezzler : defrauds :: _____ : invests
3. cancel : erase :: alter : _____
4. roads and bridges : infrastructures :: climbing a mountain : _____
5. a raise : benefit :: a broken leg : _____

Set Two

VOCABULARY LIST

jovial	asset	proliferate	prominent	propensity

6. house : _____ :: banana : fruit
7. athlete : fit :: mayor : _____
8. in a traffic jam : angry :: at a party : _____
9. pardon : forgive :: tendency : _____
10. humble : proud :: _____ : decline

Word Wise

Collocations

After her business partner left town, Tammy knew it was time to *venture out* on her own, but she was still nervous about what she would encounter. (Chapter 20)

We will display the family portrait in a *prominent place* in our new house: right over the fireplace. (Chapter 20)

Word Pairs

Asset/Liability: Asset (Chapter 20) means "a desirable thing or quality," and liability (Chapter 20) means "a disadvantage; an undesirable thing." Reynaldo's greatest asset is his friendliness; he can charm anyone. His greatest liability is his stubbornness; he won't change his mind even when he knows he is wrong.

Interesting Etymologies

Jovial (Chapter 20): comes from the Latin *Jovialis* "of Jupiter." Jupiter was the Roman god of the sky. According to astrological beliefs, those born under the sign of Jupiter were supposed to be happy people, so jovial came to mean "merry; good-humored."

Niche (Chapter 20): comes from the Latin *nidus* "nest." Or it may come from the Italian *nicchio* "seashell," which became *nicchia* "nook" and eventually *niche* in French. Today a niche has two meanings: "a recess in a wall for a decorative object," which serves as a nest for the object; and "a suitable place or position," which is what that recess in the wall was supposed to serve as.

Interactive Exercise

Imagine that have decided to become an entrepreneur. Make a brief business plan by answering the following questions.

1. Name of your business venture.

   _____

2. What does your company do or make? What is your niche in the marketplace?

   _____

   _____

3. What are two qualities you have a propensity for that would make you a successful entrepreneur?

   _____   _____

4. List two qualities that would be a big asset for your employees to have.

   _____   _____

5. Is it important that your employees be jovial? How often will they be interacting with the public?

   _____

   _____

6. List two qualities that would be a liability for your employees to have.

   _____   _____

7. What can you do to make your business prominent in your community?

   _____

   _____

8. What might you have to modify if your profits don't proliferate as you expected?

   _____

   _____

Conversation Starters

An excellent way to review the vocabulary words and help to make them your own is to use them when you are speaking. Gather three to five friends or classmates, and use one or more of the conversation starters below. Before you begin talking, have each person write down six of the vocabulary words he or she will use during the conversation. Share your lists with each other to check that you did not all pick the same six words. Try to cover all of the words you want to study, whether you are reviewing one, two, or more chapters.

1. What group do you think you would have belonged to in the Middle Ages? If time travel were possible, would you like to travel to the Middle Ages?

2. Is there an exciting piece of art or interesting building in your town?

3. How important do you think it is for people to be involved in politics? Do you vote?

4. What kind of business would you like to start? Do you think you will ever do so?

Word List

asset
[as′ et]
n. a desirable thing or quality

entrepreneur
[än′ trə prə nûr′]
n. one who assumes the risks of a business or enterprise

jovial
[jō′ vē əl]
adj. merry; good-humored; cheerful

liability
[lī′ ə bil′ i tē]
n. a disadvantage; an undesirable thing

modify
[mod′ ə fī′]
v. to change the form of; to vary; to alter partially

niche
[nich]
n. 1. an appropriate place or position
2. a recess in a wall for a statue or other decorative object

proliferate
[prə lif′ ə rāt′]
v. to increase in number; spread rapidly; to grow

prominent
[prom′ ə nənt]
adj. well known; leading; notable

propensity
[prə pen′ si tē]
n. a tendency; a leaning; a preference

venture
[ven′ chər]
n. a business enterprise; an undertaking involving risk
v. to brave; to take the risk of

Words to Watch

Which words would you like to practice with a bit more? Pick 3–5 words to study, and list them below. Write the word and its definition, and compose your own sentence using the word correctly. This extra practice could be the final touch to learning a word.

Word	Definition	Your Sentence
1. _____	_____	_____
2. _____	_____	_____
3. _____	_____	_____
4. _____	_____	_____
5. _____	_____	_____

Focus on Chapters 17–20

The following activities give you a chance to interact some more with the vocabulary words you've learned. By looking at art, taking tests, answering questions, doing a crossword puzzle, and working with others, you will see which words you know well and which you still need to work with.

Art

Match each picture below to one of the following vocabulary words. Use each word once.

VOCABULARY LIST

jovial	façade	plundering
cupola	niche	infrastructure

1. _____

2. _____

3. _____

4. _____

5. _____

6. _____

Self-Tests

1 Pick the word that best completes each sentence.

1. Kate had to _____ her exercise plans when the pool was closed for cleaning.

   a. depose   b. modify   c. plunder   d. adorn

2. Life in _____ times was difficult for most people because they had to work long hours in the fields and face the constant threat of attacks.

   a. prominent   b. medieval   c. impending   d. fertile

3. Bert's _____ attendance at college was caused by scheduling problems at his job.

   a. jovial   b. prominent   c. secular   d. intermittent

4. Some people say I have the manners of a _____, but I don't think they are that bad.

   a. liability   b. cupola   c. barbarian   d. figurehead

5. The _____ of the last college president was so disorganized that several people quit during his term.

   a. façade   b. propensity   c. regime   d. plague

2 Pick the vocabulary word that best completes the sentence. Use each word once.

a. propensity	b. feudalism	c. entrepreneur	d. coup	e. foresight

1. The military staged a _____, but their regime only lasted eight months before there was another revolt.

2. It was a system that benefited the nobles, but for most people _____ meant a life of hard work and poverty.

3. The _____ enjoyed watching her company's growth—from her garage to a new office building downtown.

4. There is a(n) _____ among students to put off writing a paper until the day before it is due.

5. Thanks to Karl's _____, we had snacks to eat when the car broke down.

3 Finish the story using the vocabulary words below. Use each word once.

VOCABULARY LIST

adorn	impending	realm	plague	assets	venture
alliance	liability	endowed	zenith	fresco	proclaimed

FLOWERS AND MORE FLOWERS

Last year I decided to (1)_____ into the flower-show

world. My neighbors had always (2)_____ my

garden the best looking on the block. I am lucky to be

(3)_____ with a green thumb. Whatever I touch grows

beautifully. Problems with pests or over- or under-watering

never (4)_____ me as they do other gardeners I know.

I have always felt that one of my (5)_____ is talking to

my plants. Only people really involved in the (6)_____

of gardening seem to understand what I mean by communicat-

ing with plants. I feel lucky to be able to (7)_____ my

living room with flowers from my garden all year long—

whether it is tulips in the spring or poinsettias in the winter.

To get ready for the (8)_____ tri-cities garden

show, I joined a(n) (9)_____ of gardeners in my

area. We exchanged ideas about the best flowers to take to

the show and how to creatively display them. The biggest

(10)_____ I had was my own pride. I thought all

of my flowers were award winners, and I had a difficult time

trying to decide which two to display (that is as many as

each person was allowed to bring). I don't know if it was

quite the (11)_____ of my life as a gardener, but I

was extremely proud when my lilies won first place.

Next year I plan to take on a completely different

challenge. I've always enjoyed art, and I hear the tri-cities

is going to have a(n) (12)_____-painting contest. I'd better find a few walls to start practicing on.

Interactive Exercise

Answer the following questions to further test your understanding of the vocabulary words.

1. What are two behaviors a ruler would have to exhibit that would stimulate people to depose him or her?

_____

_____

2. What are two prominent challenges in your life right now?

_____

_____

3. What are two reasons a person's problems might proliferate?

_____

_____

4. To whom do people usually pay homage? _____

5. Who were three charismatic leaders in history?

_____

_____

6. Whom would it be a privilege for you to meet? _____

7. What are two ways to get fertile ideas for a creative project like writing a short story or designing a painting?

_____

_____

8. If you lived during the Renaissance, do you think you would more likely be a sculptor, painter, inventor, or scientist? Why?

_____

_____

9. What are two secular activities you enjoy?

_____

_____

10. Under what conditions do you think a company would hire someone as a figurehead instead of letting the person have real control?

_____

_____

11. Why do you think humanism became popular during the Renaissance?

_____

_____

12. What kind of reading material would someone have to wrest out of your hands?

_____

_____

Crossword Puzzle

Across

3. Let's put the statue there.
4. a widespread disease
8. knowledge of the future
11. a dome
12. an agreement to cooperate
14. forecast for off-and-on rain
16. the Vikings did this
17. the highest point
18. I'm happy to donate $50,000 to the new stadium.
19. a savage

Down

1. of the Middle Ages
2. My deadline is near!
4. a tendency
5. merry and cheerful
6. bridges and roads
7. a revolt
9. a false appearance
10. government
13. Let's brave the snow and go to a movie.
15. to change the form of

Use the following words to complete the crossword puzzle. Use each word once.

VOCABULARY LIST

alliance	jovial
barbarian	medieval
coup	modify
cupola	niche
endow	plague
façade	plunder
foresight	propensity
impending	regime
infrastructure	venture
intermittent	zenith

Mix It Up

Motivating with Music

If you enjoy music, select some of your favorite tunes and get together with four or five classmates to see how music can aid in learning. Besides the music, you will need something to play it on, paper, and pens.

Decide on which words you want to study. If you are reviewing several chapters, each person should pick different vocabulary words to use so the group can cover more of the words. While the music plays, write a story that the music inspires using six or seven of the words to be studied (you may choose to write six or seven sentences each using a vocabulary word instead of writing a story). The ideas for the story or sentences may come from the tone of the music or the thoughts expressed in a song's lyrics. Share your stories or sentences with each other, and discuss the ideas the music brought out in relation to the vocabulary words. It is interesting to hear the similarities and differences the music inspires within the group. To review more words, pick another piece of music and do the activity again.

Classical music works well, but music related to a chapter may also serve as inspiration and possibly as a memory aid. For example, use medieval music for relating to Chapter 17, Renaissance music for Chapter 18, British music from the Victorian era or music from Africa for Chapter 19, and Bachman-Turner Overdrive's "Takin' Care of Business" or other songs that deal with work or business for Chapter 20. Have fun exploring how music, writing, and learning vocabulary can be creatively combined.

Exploring Alternatives

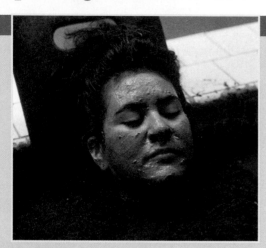

Holistic medicine has recently captured the public's interest. Health care that treats the whole individual and that often relies on alternative techniques is now appealing to a broader range of people. As people
5   begin to feel that drugs have been overprescribed, they often start searching for **naturopathic** alternatives such as herbal supplements, exercise programs, acupuncture, mud or mineral baths, and massage therapy. More and more people are investigating these
10 and other alternative methods to treat problems such as headaches, depression, breathing difficulties, and **anemia** or other weaknesses.

What many people see as a **deficiency** in traditional medicine is its inability to deal with the mind and body.
15 Massage has been found to soothe both areas, which has made it popular in alternative medicine. Once the sole **domain** of the wealthy, massage is now used in athletics, medicine, and even the workplace. Athletes have embraced massage as a way to prevent injuries
20 and to reduce soreness after exercising; medicine has used massage to deal with arthritis and back and neck pains among other problems. When employers discovered that workers are more productive when they aren't stressed, some began to hire masseuses to
25 give back and shoulder rubs in the office.

Another field that has gained popularity is aromatherapy. People have found the use of scented oils to be the **antidote** for problems such as

headaches and nervousness. Of the five senses, smell is the sharpest for most people. The oils are made from a   30
variety of plants, flowers, and herbs. Aromatherapists can combine different oils to treat a patient's problem. For example, rosemary and olive oil can be used to relieve muscle pains. The oils are usually applied during a massage, used in a bath, or inhaled.   35

As **longevity** becomes more likely for most Americans, looking at a variety of ways to treat health problems makes sense. Data from the year 2000 census estimated the average life span for males as 74.1 years and for females 79.5 years. In 1950 the   40
average life span for both sexes was 68.2 years and in 2000 the average was 76.9. In just fifty years life expectancy has gone up 8.7 years. Obviously, if the trend continues, many people can expect to lead longer lives in the years to come.   45

Some insurance companies are also beginning to see that every **syndrome** or disease isn't best treated with a pill, and they are covering more naturopathic treatments in their policies. An **eclectic** approach to health care that combines traditional and   50
nontraditional treatments may be the standard medical practice in the next decade. Patients do, however, need to choose wisely and look at the positive and negative aspects of holistic treatments before they begin any program. If the public and doctors work   55
together to find the best method of caring for a person's condition, society will benefit from an **unparalleled** era of healing.

Predicting

For each set, write the definition on the line next to the word to which it belongs. If you are unsure, return to the reading on page 138, and underline any context clues you find. After you've made your predictions, check your answers against the Word List on page 143. Place a checkmark in the box next to each word whose definition you missed. These are the words you'll want to study closely.

Set One

an area of concern	treating diseases without drugs	focusing on the importance of the whole
shortage	a lack of oxygen-carrying material in the blood, which results in weakness	

- ☐ 1. **holistic** (line 1) _____
- ☐ 2. **naturopathic** (line 6) _____
- ☐ 3. **anemia** (line 12) _____
- ☐ 4. **deficiency** (line 13) _____
- ☐ 5. **domain** (line 17) _____

Set Two

long life	diverse	without equal	a cure	a set of symptoms that belong to a disorder

- ☐ 6. **antidote** (line 28) _____
- ☐ 7. **longevity** (line 36) _____
- ☐ 8. **syndrome** (line 47) _____
- ☐ 9. **eclectic** (line 49) _____
- ☐ 10. **unparalleled** (line 58) _____

Self-Tests

1 Write the letter of the vocabulary word next to the situation that relates to it. Context clues are underlined to help you. Use each word once.

Set One

_____ 1. These doctors look at the <u>whole person</u>, not just the symptom.　　　　a. eclectic

_____ 2. You can select <u>from a variety</u> of treatments to find what works best for you.　　b. deficiency

_____ 3. I want <u>to live to be one hundred!</u>　　　　c. longevity

_____ 4. The doctor said I'm <u>low in the B vitamins and iron.</u>　　　　d. holistic

_____ 5. A monthly massage proved <u>to be the cure</u> for Sam's stress.　　　　e. antidote

Set Two

_____ 6. Mary Ann looked pale, and she <u>had no energy or strength</u>.

_____ 7. The doctor tries <u>different treatments besides prescription medication</u>.

_____ 8. If a woman drinks alcohol during pregnancy, the baby may be born <u>with certain symptoms</u>.

_____ 9. The results of my treatment with Dr. Tan are <u>so much better</u> than what I've gotten from other doctors!

_____ 10. I was surprised that aromatherapy was <u>in the realm of</u> holistic health care.

f. unparalleled

g. domain

h. syndrome

i. anemia

j. naturopathic

2 Fill in each blank with the appropriate vocabulary word. Use each word once.

VOCABULARY LIST

domain	anemia	holistic	eclectic	naturopathic
syndrome	deficiency	longevity	unparalleled	antidote

Set One

Jay couldn't figure out why he constantly felt tired and had no energy. He also suffered from pain in his joints and wasn't sleeping well. His regular physician, Dr. Gaines, found nothing wrong except a slight case of (1) _____, which she treated with iron tablets. Jay felt stronger, but he still didn't get much relief. He and his wife decided it was time to try a(n) (2) _____ health expert, a doctor who would look at the whole picture, not just the symptoms. Jay visited Dr. Sidney's clinic in March and was given a number of medical tests. Jay told the doctor that he had always been an energetic person and that laziness had never been part of his (3) _____. She told Jay that the tests would help to show whether he might be suffering from some sort of (4) _____ in an essential vitamin or mineral. After careful study, Dr. Sidney found that Jay was suffering from chronic fatigue (5) _____.

Set Two

Dr. Zhao Lee, Dr. Sidney's partner, is an expert in holistic medicine who prefers (6) _____ treatments to traditional medicine. Among his (7) _____ methods are Chinese herbal remedies, massage, and meditation. One of his patients, a sixty-five-year-old woman, was concerned about her (8) _____. She didn't think she would live much longer because of multiple allergies, and she rarely went out of the house. After doing a complete checkup, Dr. Lee found that the woman's home contained substances that were causing her allergies. He recommended immediate changes in her living environment as the first (9) _____ to her problems. She would then begin a series of physical activities that would increase as she became stronger. After four months, the woman called Dr. Lee's plan a(n) (10) _____ success. She has been extremely satisfied and has referred others to the clinic.

3 Finish the following analogies. See Completing Analogies on page 6 for instructions and practice. Use each word once.

VOCABULARY LIST

eclectic	longevity	antidote	deficiency	holistic
anemia	syndrome	domain	naturopathic	unparalleled

1. huge : immense :: diverse : _____
2. a power failure : dead phone lines :: eating healthy : _____
3. elephant : large animal :: acupuncture : _____ treatment
4. lost : ask directions :: _____ : look for a cure
5. disappointed : pleased :: _____ : abundance
6. gain twenty pounds : go on a diet :: dissatisfaction with traditional medicine : _____ treatment
7. starving : cat :: poisoned : _____
8. polka : dance :: Web site address : _____
9. lack of studying : bad grades :: _____ : weakness
10. faithful : reliable :: _____ : superior

Word Wise

Internet Activity: For Further Reading and Research

When the readings in this text capture your attention, you can turn to the Internet for more information. When you see a vocabulary word you have been studying on a Web site, note how it is used. You will also likely come across new words where you can practice your context-clue skills to discover a meaning. Here are a few sites to get you started in your quest for more information.

- For more on the Middle Ages, the Renaissance, or the Victorian era, try www.historychannel.com. At the History Channel's Web site, type in the time period or person you are interested in, and you'll have a choice of several articles to click on. See what interests you most.

- For information on endangered animals, visit the World Wildlife Fund site at www.worldwildlife.org, or the U.S. Fish and Wildlife Service page at http://endangered.fws.gov. To read over the Red List, try the International Union for Conservation of Nature site at www.iucn.org.

- To find out more about a variety of health-related issues in the United States and worldwide, go to www.nih.gov for the National Institutes of Health or www.who.int/en for the World Health Organization.

If you find any interesting sites related to the readings, share them with your classmates. Just remember to limit your time on the Internet so that you can meet all of your responsibilities.

Interactive Exercise

Imagine that you have been feeling stressed and tired lately, so you decide to visit a holistic spa or clinic for a weekend of treatments. Write a letter to a friend who is also experiencing stress inviting him or her to join you. Describe the symptoms that are prompting you to make this trip and the treatments you hope to experience. Imagine that the spa/clinic provides an eclectic blend of treatments such as acupuncture, mud baths, aromatherapy, stress management workshops, and massage therapy. Use at least six of the vocabulary words in your letter.

Dear _____ ,

_____

_____

_____

_____

_____

_____

_____

_____

_____

_____

_____

_____

Yours truly,

_____

Word Part Reminder

Below are a few short exercises to help you review the word parts you have been learning. Fill in the missing word part from the list, and circle the meaning of the word part found in each sentence. Try to complete the questions without returning to the Word Parts chapter. This reminder focuses on roots from all three Word Parts chapters. Refer to the Word Parts list on the inside back cover to find the page number if you need to look back at any of the chapters.

vent	vert	cred	fin

1. It was a good thing I decided to turn my coffee cup over. If I had not in_____ed it, I might have been tempted to drink more than I should have the next time the waitress came by with the pot.

2. I could no longer believe Jenny when she told me the in_____ible story that she was late because she had been captured by aliens.

3. I decided to limit myself to one piece of candy a day. For the first week, I found it really hard to con_____e myself to such a small amount.

4. So far we know that 300 people are going to come to the con_____ion this summer.

Word List

anemia
[ə nē′ mē ə]
n. a lack of oxygen-carrying material in the blood, which results in weakness

antidote
[an′ ti dōt′]
n. 1. something that prevents an unwanted effect; a cure
2. a medicine or other remedy for counteracting the effects of a poison or a disease

deficiency
[di fish′ ən sē]
n. lack; shortage

domain
[dō mān′]
n. 1. an area of concern; a field
2. a territory of control; a realm

eclectic
[i klek′ tik]
adj. selecting from various sources; diverse

holistic
[hō lis′ tik]
adj. 1. focusing on the importance of the whole and how its parts depend on each other
2. nontraditional health care

longevity
[lon jev′ i tē, lôn-]
n. long life; length of life or service

naturopathic
[nā chər′ ə path′ ik]
adj. treating diseases without drugs

syndrome
[sin′ drōm, -drəm]
n. a set of symptoms that belong to a disorder or disease

unparalleled
[un par′ ə leld′]
adj. unmatched; without equal

Words to Watch

Which words would you like to practice with a bit more? Pick 3–5 words to study, and list them below. Write the word and its definition, and compose your own sentence using the word correctly. This extra practice could be the final touch to learning a word.

Word	Definition	Your Sentence
1.		
2.		
3.		
4.		
5.		

23

City Planning

Public Input

Upcoming Design Meeting

We invite the public's input on a proposal for the renewal of the 22nd block of Evergreen Avenue. The plan calls for condominiums, office space, and retail shops to occupy the block. The plan is currently called Evergreen Plaza. The goal is to bring people back to the **urban** center and create a community where people can live, work, shop, and play. For the last thirty years, people have been steadily movingout of the downtown core for the suburbs. With the increases in traffic congestion and higher gas prices, many people are no longer willing to **endure** long commutes and the hassles associated with living outside of the city. To **rectify** this problem, we are creating a downtown people will want to live in. We encourage people to discover the numerous rewards of city living.

The **edifice** we are proposing will meet a variety of needs. We have conducted several surveys to get a **consensus** on the services people desire in downtown living. People agreed that they wanted places to relax. The twelve-story residential building will feature a rooftop garden with **panoramic** views of the bay and surrounding mountains and plenty of chairs to lounge on and take in the views. There will also be a space where people can tend their own small garden plots to grow fresh fruits and vegetables. The entire complex will be designed with green areas where people can relax in the shade of a tree or enjoy the serenity found in listening to a nearby fountain. People also indicated that they wanted a sense of community. A central room on the seventh floor will give residents a place to chat, play pool or ping pong, and watch movies on a large-screen television. People wanted the convenience of shopping close by. A four-story, mixed-use building on the site will provide a grocery, coffee bar, restaurants, and specialty stores. There will also be an eight-story office building, so residents may not even need to leave the block to go to work. Glass and steal will be combined for an open feel to the offices and residences. The buildings will exemplify the best and latest in green technology and energy-efficient systems, including solar and wind power.

Evergreen Plaza will be a **gateway** to downtown attractions. From here residents can easily walk or use public transportation to visit many of downtown's sights, including the art museum, science center, aquarium, and ball park. Several movie and live theaters are within a three-block walk. As the city works to **revitalize** downtown, Evergreen Plaza will play a prominent role in the process. We consider our design the **definitive** answer to our city's need to grow in an environmentally and people-friendly manner.

The meeting will **convene** Thursday, April 23, at 6 p.m. at City Hall. During the first hour, a synopsis of the plans as well as sketches of the interiors and exteriors of the proposed buildings and photographs of the types of plants and fountains we plan to install will be presented. We will begin eliciting comments and questions from the public at seven. We eagerly await your advice as we move onto phase two of this exciting project.

Predicting

For each set, write the definition on the line next to the word to which it belongs. If you are unsure, return to the reading on page 144, and underline any context clues you find. After you've made your predictions, check your answers against the Word List on page 149. Place a checkmark in the box next to each word whose definition you missed. These are the words you'll want to study closely.

Set One

a building or a structure   to correct   agreement   to tolerate   concerned with a city

☐ 1. **urban** (line 4) _____

☐ 2. **endure** (line 6) _____

☐ 3. **rectify** (line 7) _____

☐ 4. **edifice** (line 9) _____

☐ 5. **consensus** (line 10) _____

Set Two

most reliable or complete   to renew   scenic   something that functions as an entrance   to assemble

☐ 6. **panoramic** (line 12) _____

☐ 7. **gateway** (line 27) _____

☐ 8. **revitalize** (line 31) _____

☐ 9. **definitive** (line 32) _____

☐ 10. **convene** (line 34) _____

Self-Tests

1 Find the synonym or definition in each sentence and replace it by writing the corresponding vocabulary word on the blank line. Use each word once.

VOCABULARY LIST				
endure	revitalize	panoramic	consensus	urban
definitive	gateway	edifice	convene	rectify

1. I like the city life, but sometimes it is nice to get out in the countryside. _____

2. The salesman had to tolerate several doors slammed in his face before he made his first sale. _____

3. The view from the top of the mountain was scenic. _____

4. I wasn't sure how to fix the problem, so I talked to my boss about possible solutions. _____

5. The concert hall is the largest and grandest building in town. _____

VOCABULARY LIST

endure	revitalize	panoramic	consensus	urban
definitive	gateway	edifice	convene	rectify

6. Everyone is going to meet at my house, and then we will carpool to the play. _____

7. When I want the most reliable information on how to fix my car, I go to my dad. He has been working on cars for fifty years. _____

8. We were able to reach an agreement on what to get grandma for her 90th birthday after an hour of discussing possible gifts. _____

9. When I heard that the town of Worthington was going to invigorate its downtown, I didn't expect it to look like a Swiss village. _____

10. A trip to an amusement park is the way to enter a world of fun and adventure. _____

2 Finish the sentences about some of the world's most amazing edifices. Use each word once.

VOCABULARY LIST

convene	revitalized	panoramic	consensus	edifice
definitive	gateway	endure	urban	rectify

1. Efforts to _____ problems with portions of the Great Wall in China have run into problems due to official procedures.

2. The Empire State building has been a part of New York City's _____ skyline since the 1930s.

3. After initial mixed reviews, Australians have reached a _____ that the Sydney Opera House is a building to be proud of.

4. Suggestions that parts of Machu Picchu be _____ to show what it looked like at the time of the Incas have been firmly turned down.

5. The Arch in St. Louis is a _____ to the West.

6. The Eiffel Tower offers _____ views of Paris.

7. There is still no _____ answer on how the pyramids in Egypt were built.

8. The Sears Tower in Chicago is the tallest _____ in the United States.

9. Visitors often have to _____ heat and long lines to tour the Taj Mahal in India, but the magnificence of the building makes the hardships worth it.

10. On New Year's Eve, people in Seattle _____ at the foot of the Space Needle to watch fireworks shoot from the top of it.

3 For each set, write the letter of the most logical analogy. See Completing Analogies on page 6 for instructions and practice.

Set One

_____ 1. last : endure ::

_____ 2. arch : gateway ::

_____ 3. spatula : to turn a pancake ::

_____ 4. neglected buildings : revitalize ::

_____ 5. dark : light ::

a. dictionary : to find definitive spellings

b. disagreement : consensus

c. ball : toy

d. feeling ill : visit a doctor

e. combination : mixture

Set Two

_____ 6. musician : performs ::

_____ 7. pants : clothing ::

_____ 8. quit : stop ::

_____ 9. worsen : rectify ::

_____ 10. a meadow : panoramic ::

f. a street : busy

g. mansion : edifice

h. lovely : ugly

i. meeting : convenes

j. city : urban

Word Wise

Collocations

There is a definite *deficiency in* math skills among the latest graduating class; only 33% passed the state exam. (Chapter 22)

The fund-raiser was an *unparalleled success.* We generated almost $70,000. (Chapter 22)

After three hours of discussion, the committee *reached a consensus* on whom to invite as the main speaker for the conference. (Chapter 23)

The story of the alligator that crawls out of the sewer and eats a baby is an *urban legend.* (Chapter 23)

Interesting Etymologies

Consensus (Chapter 23): comes from the Latin *consentire,* "feel together." It is made up of *com-,* "with," plus *sentire,* "to feel." When people "feel together," or the same way, they illustrate the definition of consensus: "agreement; harmony."

Panorama (Chapter 23): comes from the Greek *pan* meaning "all or every" and *horan,* "to see." Thus, a panorama is "a view over a wide area," and panoramic is "a wide view" with the additional idea that this view is "scenic or pleasing."

Interactive Exercise

Answer the following questions as if you are the city planner. You can use the city you live in to develop your answers or create a fictitious city. Use at least two of the vocabulary words in each response.

1. What is the biggest problem in your urban area? What can you do to rectify it?

   _____

   _____

   _____

2. What kind of new edifice does your city need most? Why? Do you think there would be a consensus among the citizens about your decision?

   _____

   _____

   _____

3. What kind of problems might you have to endure as you revitalize the downtown area?

   _____

   _____

   _____

4. Do you need to design a building, plaza, or park to give people a better place to convene? What could it have a panoramic view of?

   _____

   _____

   _____

5. What kind of building, sculpture, or monument would best serve as a gateway to the downtown? Why would your idea be considered the definitive choice?

   _____

   _____

   _____

HINT

A Comfortable Spot

To concentrate on what you are reading, you need to find the right environment. For most people that means turning off the television and radio. Most people concentrate better in a quiet space. You can experiment to see if you are the kind of person who actually concentrates better with some background noise. Also look for a place with good light; you don't want to strain your eyes. You should be comfortable, so find a chair you like, or, if you need to take notes, you may want to sit at a table. For some people, especially if they are reading for fun, sitting outside in a park or the back yard provides a pleasant place to read. See what works best for you depending on what material you are reading. Change your environment if you find you can't focus on what you are reading.

Word List

consensus
[kən sen′ səs]

n. unity of opinion;
agreement; harmony

convene
[kən vēn′]

v. 1. to assemble, usually
for a public purpose;
to organize
2. to summon to appear

definitive
[di fin′ ə tiv]

adj. most reliable or
complete

edifice
[e′ də fis]

n. a building or a structure,
usually used when
referring to a large or
important building

endure
[en door′, -dyoor′, in-]

v. 1. to tolerate; to allow
2. to last

gateway
[gāt′ wā]

n. 1. something that functions
as an entrance or point
of entry
2. a structure around an
entrance that can be
shut by a gate

panoramic
[pan′ ə ram′ ik]

adj. a wide view; scenic
or pleasing

rectify
[rek′ tə fī]

v. to correct; to put
right; to fix

revitalize
[rē vīt′ l īz′]

v. to renew; to invigorate;
to refresh

urban
[ûr′ bən]

adj. 1. concerned with
a city
2. typical of a city or
city life

Words to Watch

Which words would you like to practice with a bit more? Pick 3–5 words to study, and list them below.
Write the word and its definition, and compose your own sentence using the word correctly. This extra
practice could be the final touch to learning a word.

Word	Definition	Your Sentence
1. _____	_____	_____
2. _____	_____	_____
3. _____	_____	_____
4. _____	_____	_____
5. _____	_____	_____

Psychology

Therapy Notes

		Session 6
		We continued exploring Greta's alternate personalities.
		Today she revealed the presence of Maria, who suffers from
		a cleaning **obsession**. She took a handkerchief out of Greta's
	5	purse and began dusting the couch and lamp as we talked.
		She told me that she liked everything to be neat and tidy
		and that she couldn't relax if there was a speck of dust
		around. Greta's **ego** continues to be quite fragile. She doesn't like to talk about her life from the ages
		of seven to thirteen. I sense, as I meet each of her alternate personalities, that I'm getting closer to
	10	discovering the childhood secret Greta feels the need to **suppress**.
		Session 8
		Greta experienced another lost-time episode over the weekend. Her **amnesia** seems to be related to a
		wedding she had told me she was to attend. Her best friend was getting married, but Greta remem-
		bers nothing about being at the wedding, though she brought me candy wrapped in lace that appears
	15	to be a wedding favor. The stress of the wedding may have been what brought out Lily. Lily surprised
		me by speaking with a French accent. She talked about the numerous cocktails she drank over the
		weekend and vividly described her encounter with a man she'd met at a bar. Lily clearly represents
		Greta's **id**. Lily also indicated that **voyeurism** is a part of her personality. She spoke about watching
		the man across the street through binoculars, and she got quite excited when she mentioned his
	20	activities with a woman. If Lily often takes over, Greta's host body may be in great danger. I asked
		Greta to tell me about a dream she recently had. She shared a dramatic dream about floating above
		her childhood home. There was a huge dragon that kept blowing fire at her. We looked at the possible
		subliminal meanings the dream could be conveying about her relationship with her parents.
		Session 12
	25	I spent the first half of the session calming Sybil's **hysteria**. She kept shouting that she was "cramped."
		Her outburst seems to stem from **claustrophobia**. My office is small, but I had never considered it
		that confining. Harriet then emerged. She is the sixth personality I have met; I've read of cases where
		people have had ten different personalities. Harriet was quite proper in speech, and she fastened the
		top button of Greta's blouse before acknowledging me. She has very clear ideas on correct behavior.
	30	She was vaguely aware of and disapproving of Lily. Harriet obviously represents Greta's **superego**. I
		decided to show Greta a few inkblots to see if they might help to reveal what she is repressing. Greta
		finally spoke of physical abuse she suffered from her parents as a child. Today was a major
		breakthrough!

Predicting

For each set, write the definition on the line next to the word to which it belongs. If you are unsure, return to the reading on page 150, and underline any context clues you find. After you've made your predictions, check your answers against the Word List on page 155. Place a checkmark in the box next to each word whose definition you missed. These are the words you'll want to study closely.

Set One

the pleasure-loving, aggressive part of a person   loss of memory   to repress   self-esteem

an idea that excessively occupies the mind

❑   1.   **obsession** (line 4 _____

❑   2.   **ego** (line 8) _____

❑   3.   **suppress** (line 10) _____

❑   4.   **amnesia** (line 12) _____

❑   5.   **id** (line 18) _____

Set Two

understandable by the subconscious   the act of watching others   a fear of small or enclosed places

the moralistic part of a person   nervous outburst

❑   6.   **voyeurism** (line 18) _____

❑   7.   **subliminal** (line 23) _____

❑   8.   **hysteria** (line 25) _____

❑   9.   **claustrophobia** (line 26) _____

❑   10.   **superego** (line 30) _____

Self-Tests

1 Match each vocabulary word with the words that could be associated with it.

Word Associations

_____	1. suppress	a. aggressive, angry
_____	2. superego	b. small, fear
_____	3. voyeurism	c. hold back, repress
_____	4. amnesia	d. underneath, secretive
_____	5. hysteria	e. looking, peeking
_____	6. id	f. forgetfulness, memory loss

_____ 7. subliminal   g. constant, fixation

_____ 8. obsession   h. outburst, confusion

_____ 9. ego   i. uptight, moral

_____ 10. claustrophobia   j. personality, self

2 Finish the headlines with the vocabulary words. Use each word once.

VOCABULARY LIST

obsession	superego	amnesia	ego	hysteria
suppresses	id	subliminal	voyeurism	claustrophobia

---

1. *Woman's _____ with Ancient Greece Leads to Book Deal About Her Experiences*

2. _____ on the Rise: Five People Arrested Over the Weekend for Peeking in Windows

3. Top Athlete's _____ Hurt When Beat by Ten-Year-Old

4. People Who Suffer from _____ Advised to Avoid "Tiny Spaces" Art Exhibit

5. Man Reunited with Family After His _____ Cured

6. Suspected _____ Messages in Children's Cartoons Under Investigation

7. New Regime _____ Unfavorable Newspaper Articles

8. *Crowd's _____ at Shopping Mall Opening Leads to Police Intervention*

9. Scientists Examine the Role of the _____ in Teaching Children Morals

10. Overactive _____ Blamed for Barroom Fight

3 Pretend you are engaged in the following activities, and match each to the word it suggests.

VOCABULARY LIST				
ego	subliminal	id	amnesia	suppress
superego	claustrophobia	hysteria	voyeurism	obsession

1. You can't remember a thing about the last two weeks. _____
2. You are relaxing in the sun while eating a huge slice of chocolate cake. _____
3. You tell yourself, "Stand up straight" and "Don't touch." _____
4. Your subconscious sees a skull on a bottle in an alcohol advertisement. _____
5. You look through binoculars at the man undressing in the apartment across the street. _____
6. You keep storing old newspapers in your garage even though you have no use for them. _____
7. You stop yourself from eating a second slice of pie. _____
8. You are afraid of getting into an elevator. _____
9. This is your reaction when you can't find your seven-year-old at the beach. _____
10. You are told that you did an excellent job on a paper. _____

Word Wise

Collocations

In marketing class, we examined a whiskey ad that was filled with *subliminal messages* that only the subconscious could detect. (Chapter 24)

Interesting Etymologies

Claustrophobia (Chapter 24): comes from the Latin *claustrum,* "a place shut in," which comes from *claudere,* "to close." With the addition of the Greek *phobos,* "fear," claustrophobia means "a fear of small or enclosed places." The word was first used in the *British Medical Journal* in 1879.

Obsession (Chapter 24): comes from the Latin *obsessio,* "to occupy." In the past, it referred to an evil spirit that was trying to take over or occupy a person. Today the meaning is not as supernatural; it is "an idea that excessively occupies the mind."

Interactive Exercise ||||||||||||||||||||||||||||||||||||||||||||||||||||||||||||||||||||||||||||||||||

Pick two of the inkblots, and write a paragraph about what you see in the blots using at least three vocabulary words in each paragraph. You may need to use your imagination to find some meaning in the blots.

PARAGRAPH 1

Inkblot # _____   _____

_____

_____

_____

_____

_____

PARAGRAPH 2

Inkblot # _____   _____

_____

_____

_____

_____

_____

HINT

Play Games with Words

To make reading and vocabulary fun, learn to enjoy using words in recreational contexts.

- Pick up the Sunday paper, and do the crossword puzzle.
- Buy popular board games that are based on using words such as Scrabble, Boggle, or Scattergories. Invite your friends over to play.
- Play simple word games when traveling—for example, using words that are at least five letters long, the first person says a word and the next person must say a word that begins with the last letter of the previous word: backward, doctor, rabbit, talking, girls.
- Write cards, letters, or e-mail messages that play with language—for example, write a thank-you note that uses several synonyms to express what a "great" time you had: wonderful, magnificent, fabulous, marvelous. Your friends will enjoy getting your letters or e-mail.

Word List

amnesia
[am nē′ zhə]
n. loss of memory, often from an illness or shock; forgetfulness

claustrophobia
[klô′ strə fō′ bē ə]
n. a fear of small or enclosed places

ego
[ē′ gō]
n. the conscious part of a person; self-esteem

hysteria
[hi ster′ ē ə]
n. emotional excess; nervous outburst; excitement

id
[id]
n. the primitive, pleasure-loving, aggressive part of a person

obsession
[əb sesh′ ən, ob-]
n. an idea that excessively occupies the mind; a fascination

subliminal
[sub lim′ ə nəl]
adj. understandable by the subconscious; hidden

superego
[soo′ pər ē′ go]
n. the moralistic part of a person

suppress
[sə pres′]
v. 1. to consciously inhibit an impulse or action; to repress
2. to abolish; to conquer
3. to withhold from publication; to censor

voyeurism
[vwä yûr′ iz əm]
n. the act of watching others, especially secretively and usually related to sexual objects or acts

Words to Watch

Which words would you like to practice with a bit more? Pick 3–5 words to study, and list them below. Write the word and its definition, and compose your own sentence using the word correctly. This extra practice could be the final touch to learning a word.

Word	Definition	Your Sentence
1.		
2.		
3.		
4.		
5.		

© 2010 Pearson Education, Inc.

25

Drama

All the World's a Stage

Last week the 22nd annual Summer Theater Festival opened to much **acclaim**. As in the past, the praise given to the plays is justly earned. Last weekend I viewed all three shows and was thrilled with them.

5   First I saw *Oedipus Rex* by the great Greek dramatist Sophocles. For the Greeks, going to the theater was part of a religious ritual meant to cleanse their souls. Today the experience is not so deep for most of us, but a good play can still bring

10 about a **catharsis**. I felt some of my tensions released as I witnessed the ordeals poor Oedipus faced. It is a play that will make you **pensive**. There is so much to reflect on from the dangers of pride to what fate has in store for us. While watching the play, I recalled the Greek **credo**: "Know thyself, nothing in excess." It is an excellent system of

15 belief but a hard one to always follow, as Oedipus reminds us.

     For a lighter theater experience, I next attended Shakespeare's *As You Like It*. It was fun to watch the couples chase love as they frolicked in the Forest of Arden. Nell Gwyn's performance as Rosalind is **transcendent**. I have never seen such energy brought to the role; I felt like I had been transported to the forest myself. The director has also wisely chosen to use some **subtle** movements between

20 Rosalind and Orlando that will allow the careful observer to better appreciate the workings of their relationship. And the colorful costumes add much to the play, especially the women's disguises.

     Finally, I attended the debut of the **avant-garde** play *The Painter's Smile*. Rumor has it that one of our country's famous playwrights wasn't sure how audiences would respond to the play so she used a **pseudonym**. If the rumors are true, she needn't have worried; she could have easily put her real name on

25 this one. Though the play won't appeal to everyone because of its experimental nature, it is still a fine piece of drama with lines that will make you laugh and scenes that will make you cry. The main character has a moving **soliloquy** on his relationship with his parents that brought quite a few tears to the house. I thought if only he had expressed those ideas to his parents, the play would have had quite a different

30 ending. The **finale** is worth mentioning—it is quite unusual. The audience is warned not to wear their best clothes as paint plays a role in the last moments of the play. Large bibs are even handed out to audience members who want to cover up. I won't say

35 more; you'll have to experience it yourself.

     I have no misgivings in recommending these three plays to you. Before the summer ends, treat yourself to a fantastic theater experience by seeing one or more of the plays. They will be running until

40 the end of August. Call (714) 555-5423 for more information, or check online at theaterfest.org.

Predicting

For each set, write the definition on the line next to the word to which it belongs. If you are unsure, return to the reading on page 156, and underline any context clues you find. After you've made your predictions, check your answers against the Word List on page 161. Place a checkmark in the box next to each word whose definition you missed. These are the words you'll want to study closely.

Set One

| superior | the relief of emotional tensions | thoughtful | a formula of belief | enthusiastic approval or praise |

- ❏ 1. **acclaim** (line 2) _____
- ❏ 2. **catharsis** (line 10) _____
- ❏ 3. **pensive** (line 12) _____
- ❏ 4. **credo** (line 14) _____
- ❏ 5. **transcendent** (line 18) _____

Set Two

| experimental | the concluding part of any performance | not obvious | a fictitious name |
a speech in which a character, alone or as if alone, expresses innermost thoughts

- ❏ 6. **subtle** (line 19) _____
- ❏ 7. **avant-garde** (line 22) _____
- ❏ 8. **pseudonym** (line 24) _____
- ❏ 9. **soliloquy** (line 27) _____
- ❏ 10. **finale** (line 30) _____

Self-Tests

1 Match the quotation to the word it illustrates. Context clues are underlined to help you. Use each word once.

VOCABULARY LIST

| subtle | finale | acclaim | pseudonym | catharsis |

Set One

1. "Did you know Samuel Clemens used the <u>pen name</u> Mark Twain?" _____
2. "I loved <u>the end of the show</u> when the missing sister suddenly appeared and her evil twin was forced to admit what she had done." _____
3. "I cried and cried after my cat Buttons died. It felt so good <u>to let my feelings out</u>." _____
4. "I was sitting right next to my niece, and it <u>wasn't a bit obvious</u> that she took all but two of the chocolates from the tray." _____
5. "Robert, you deserve this award for all your hours of hard work and your enthusiasm for every project. <u>The whole department thanks you</u>!" _____

Set Two

6. "I embarrassed Rafael when I entered the room and heard him <u>talking to himself</u> about whether to ask Alexandra out." _____

7. "In this picture I am dancing in the streets at Carnival. You know <u>my motto</u>, 'When in Rome, do as the Romans do.'" _____

8. "I have been <u>thinking</u> all day about what to say to Colin's teacher." _____

9. "Oh! This fish is marvelous; it is <u>the best fish I have ever had</u>!" _____

10. "This new novel is definitely <u>experimental</u>. Each chapter starts at the end of an event and goes backward, so people keep coming back to life." _____

2 Complete the following sentences using the vocabulary words. Use each word once.

VOCABULARY LIST

acclaim	pensive	pseudonym	transcendent	catharsis
finale	soliloquy	avant-garde	credo	subtle

1. The sculpture was considered _____ twenty years ago, but now people see it as traditional.

2. My uncle's _____ is "life's too short—eat dessert first."

3. The child was _____ the day before starting kindergarten.

4. I have to study hard for my _____; it is my chance to shine in the play.

5. I felt _____ when I finally beat my father at bowling.

6. The design of the new courthouse earned _____ from most people.

7. Reading a funny book offered me a much needed _____ after a stressful week at work.

8. The _____ of the play took me by surprise; I couldn't believe that was how it would end.

9. Boz was the _____ Charles Dickens sometimes used.

10. The taste is _____, but I can detect a bit of cinnamon in the cookies.

3 As you read the following story, write the word that each scene suggests. Context clues are underlined to help you. Use each word once.

VOCABULARY LIST

acclaim	pseudonym	transcendent	soliloquy	avant-garde
credo	pensive	catharsis	finale	subtle

1. I had heard that the new drama *In the Meadow* was <u>superior to anything else in the theater season</u>; I had to see it. _____

2. The play opened with a man in a clown suit <u>talking to himself</u> about whether to join a circus or a cult and live underwater. _____

3. Then two women in bright yellow sheets emerged from a flower and <u>reflected</u> on the bad and good times in their lives._____

4. Next, four people wrapped in towels crossed the stage chanting, "The way to happiness is all around you." Every ten minutes they repeated this <u>belief.</u>_____

5. The woman next to me <u>laughed uncontrollably</u> and then <u>wept loudly.</u> _____

6. When the first act ended, several people <u>applauded and yelled,</u> "Bravo!" _____

7. This play was <u>very different,</u> and most of the audience seemed to like it, but I guess I am just not a fan of <u>experimental theater.</u> _____

8. I decided that, during the second act, I would work on finding <u>the meanings that were harder to see or understand,</u> and maybe then I would appreciate the play. _____

9. As I took my seat, the woman next to me whispered, "I heard the play was really written a hundred years ago by George Bernard Shaw <u>under the name</u> Bernie Higgins because he didn't think the stage was ready for such a work." I nodded and tried not to show what I thought of such a ridiculous idea. _____

10. <u>At the end of the play,</u> buckets of water fell on the whole cast, and they shouted, "The way to happiness...." The end summed up my feelings about the play, and I found my way to happiness out the front door. _____

Word Wise

Collocations

The *grand finale* at this year's symphony will include fireworks and a water show. (Chapter 25)

Connotations and Denotations

Avant-garde (Chapter 25): denotation—as an adjective, "experimental," and as a noun, "the advanced group in a field." The denotative meaning doesn't say whether the avant-garde is good or bad. The connotative meanings take in people's response to change. People who are upset by those who try new ideas or techniques can regard the avant-garde suspiciously. Connotations for avant-garde can range from an admiring group that sees the avant-garde as forward-thinkers to those who consider the avant-garde as a band of far-out people working to destroy traditions.

Interesting Etymologies

Catharsis (Chapter 25): comes from the Greek *kathairein,* "to purify; to purge." A *katharsis* for the Greeks was a "purging or cleansing." It was first used in the modern medical sense of "the relief of emotional tensions" in the late 1800s.

Interactive Exercise

Give two examples of places you might encounter each word.

EXAMPLE: *avant-garde: at a modern art museum or a hip fashion show*
pseudonym: on a note from a secret admirer or on a person's profile at a dating Web site

acclaim

1. _____ 2. _____

credo

1. _____ 2. _____

pseudonym

1. _____ 2. _____

catharsis

1. _____ 2. _____

transcendent

1. _____ 2. _____

avant-garde

1. _____ 2. _____

finale

1. _____ 2. _____

soliloquy

1. _____ 2. _____

pensive

1. _____ 2. _____

subtle

1. _____ 2. _____

Conversation Starters

An excellent way to review the vocabulary words and help to make them your own is to use them when you are speaking. Gather three to five friends or classmates, and use one or more of the conversation starters below. Before you begin talking, have each person write down six of the vocabulary words he or she will use during the conversation. Share your lists with each other to check that you did not all pick the same six words. Try to cover all of the words you want to study, whether you are reviewing one, two, or more chapters.

1. What kind of alternative medicine have you tried or would you consider trying?

2. Would you rather live in an urban or suburban environment? Why?

3. Do you think dream analysis or inkblots are helpful ways to explore the subconscious?

4. Have you ever been in a play, or would you like to be in one?

Word List

acclaim
[ə klām′]

n. enthusiastic approval or praise
v. to applaud; to announce with enthusiastic approval

avant-garde
[ä′ vänt gärd′]

adj. experimental
n. the advanced group in a field

catharsis
[kə thär′ sis]

n. the relief of emotional tensions, especially through a work of art

credo
[krē′ dō, krā′-]

n. a formula of belief; a code or ritual

finale
[fi nal′ ē, -nä′ lē]

n. the concluding part of any performance; end

pensive
[pen′ siv]

adj. thoughtful; reflective

pseudonym
[soo′ də nim′]

n. a fictitious name usually used by an author to conceal his or her identity; pen name

soliloquy
[sə lil′ ə kwē]

n. 1. a speech in a drama in which a character, alone or as if alone, expresses innermost thoughts
2. the act of talking while or as if alone

subtle
[sut′ l]

adj. 1. not obvious; hard to see
2. difficult to understand; cunning; clever

transcendent
[tran sen′ dənt]

adj. superior; going beyond ordinary limits

Words to Watch

Which words would you like to practice with a bit more? Pick 3–5 words to study, and list them below. Write the word and its definition, and compose your own sentence using the word correctly. This extra practice could be the final touch to learning a word.

Word	Definition	Your Sentence
1.		
2.		
3.		
4.		
5.		

Focus on Chapters 22–25

The following activities give you a chance to interact some more with the vocabulary words you've learned. By looking at art, taking tests, answering questions, doing a crossword puzzle, and working with others, you will see which words you know well and which you still need to work with.

Art

Match each picture below to one of the following vocabulary words. Use each word once.

VOCABULARY LIST

consensus	finale	voyeurism
claustrophobia	anemia	soliloquy

1. _____

2. _____

3. _____

4. _____

5. _____

6. _____

1 Pick the word that best completes each sentence.

1. The bank was such an impressive _____ that people felt confident leaving their money there.

   a. soliloquy   b. superego   c. deficiency   d. edifice

2. I live by the _____ "Do unto others as you would have them do unto you."

   a. domain   b. voyeurism   c. gateway   d. credo

3. I was suffering from what I referred to as Overwork _____. The symptoms include tired eyes from staring at a computer and an expanding rear end from sitting all day. I gave myself a prescription of a long weekend with lots of exercise.

   a. anemia   b. edifice   c. syndrome   d. acclaim

4. I like the concept of _____ medicine because the doctor looks at all aspects of my health.

   a. holistic   b. subliminal   c. definitive   d. claustrophobia

5. Her _____ is so big that she thought the office holiday party was to honor her birthday in December.

   a. ego   b. consensus   c. pseudonym   d. hysteria

2 Pick the vocabulary word that best completes the sentence. Use each word once.

a. definitive	b. pensive	c. naturopathic	d. transcendent	e. subliminal

1. The music was _____; it made me feel like I was dancing in the clouds.

2. I think my girlfriend is sending me _____ messages. For some reason I want to buy her a ring, but I can't logically figure out why.

3. I wanted to see a _____ doctor because I was interested in herbal treatments and acupuncture.

4. I consider *Grill the Right Way* the _____ source when I have a question about barbequing.

5. The team members were _____ before the big debate, but they knew they had thoroughly practiced and were ready for anything.

3 Finish the story using the vocabulary words below. Use each word once.

OLD AND NEW CURES

For the last year, I had been suffering from various aches and pains, but several doctors couldn't find an exact cause. The pain I sometimes had to (1) _____ was unbearable. My friend then told me about a doctor who had received great (2) _____ for her nontraditional methods. The (3) _____ of some of her patients was amazing. At least two dozen of them were over 110. Then my friend told me that I would have to travel to Mongolia, where the doctor was currently practicing. I was shocked that I would have to go so far, but I was ready to try anything to (4) _____ my problems.

I e-mailed the doctor, and she replied that treatments could begin in two months. She also asked me to describe everything that had happened to me around the time the pains had begun. That is when I recalled my (5) _____. There was a two-week period where I couldn't remember a thing that had happened to me. The doctor thought I might be (6) _____ something that happened during those two weeks. She said if I could get to her in a month, she would like to have her team begin (7) _____ with me.

When I arrived, I went immediately to the address the doctor had given me. I was surprised to find a beautiful courtyard filled with birds. The serene scene set the mood for my treatments. I felt like I was about to enter the (8) _____ of a master. I had talked to more people about the doctor before I left, and they spoke of her (9) _____ success in dealing with mysterious disorders.

At first the doctor watched me as I sat on the floor. Everything was very quiet. She later told me that she was looking for (10) _____ signs of what was wrong with me. She asked me about what was happening in my life prior to the two weeks I couldn't remember. Then she said something that surprised me. She told me that my (11) _____ was working to repress something my id had done. I wasn't expecting a psychological analysis. She laughed and said she was interested in all forms of medicine—East and West, body and mind. Over the next few days I was given herbal treatments, massages, and acupuncture. The doctor also recommended a good therapist in my hometown. The whole experience was a (12) _____. I felt so many tensions leave my body during that week. I now knew that I could deal with whatever I was suppressing and that my body would heal in the process.

Interactive Exercise ||||||||||||||||||||||||||||||||||||||||||||||||||||||||||||||

Answer the following questions to further test your understanding of the vocabulary words.

1. What is something you want to revitalize?

   _____

   _____

2. What is there a deficiency of in your life?

   _____

   _____

3. Are you a fan of the avant-garde in painting, music, drama or other art form? Explain why or why not.

   _____

   _____

4. What are two things that are a gateway to a fulfilling job?

   _____

   _____

5. If you were to use an eclectic design in your house, what styles would you pick?

   _____

   _____

6. What are two activities your id enjoys doing?

   _____

   _____

7. What do you see as three benefits to urban living?

   _____

   _____

8. What are two things people commonly have obsessions about?

   _____

   _____

9. Where would you go in your area to enjoy a panoramic view?

   _____

10. If you were going to write under a pseudonym, what name would you pick? Why?

   _____

   _____

11. What event could lead to mass hysteria?

   _____

12. In what kind of situation might a person need an antidote?

   _____

Crossword Puzzle

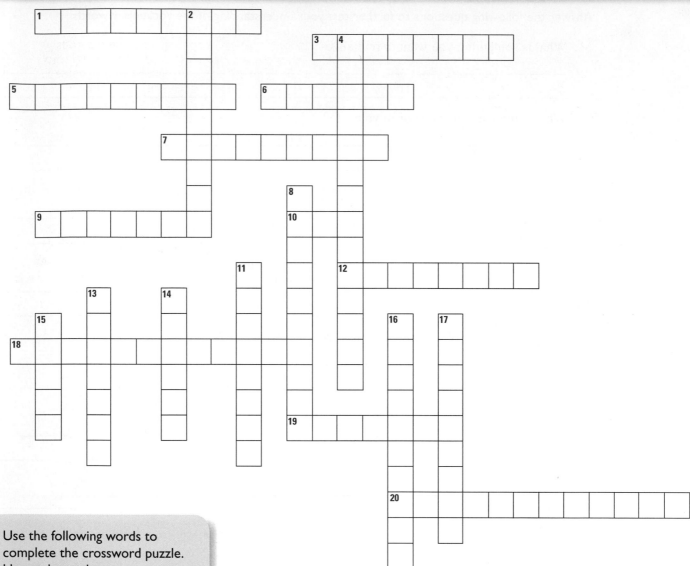

Use the following words to complete the crossword puzzle. Use each word once.

VOCABULARY LIST

anemia	finale
catharsis	holistic
claustrophobia	longevity
consensus	naturopathic
convene	rectify
credo	soliloquy
definitive	subliminal
eclectic	superego
edifice	transcendent
ego	voyeurism

Across

1. I'm glad we all agree.
3. diverse
5. the relief of emotional tensions
6. the concluding part of any performance
7. Pat peaks in people's windows.
9. to correct
10. self-esteem
12. nontraditional health care
18. superior
19. a bank or office building
20. treating disorders without drugs

Down

2. the act of talking while alone
4. fear of enclosed places
8. most reliable
11. the moralistic part of a person
13. I call this meeting to order.
14. I feel weak.
15. Live by the sword, die by the sword
16. hidden
17. living to be 120

Make Learning Fun

Think about the kinds of activities you like to do, and see if you can incorporate the traits involved in those activities into your learning experiences. If you like group activities (team sports, going to big parties), create study groups. If you like to draw, add visual elements to your notes, draw what happens in a story you read, or make a diagram to help you understand a concept. The more you enjoy what you do, whether in school or at work, the more you want to do it. Find the ways to make your life and learning fun.

Mix It Up

Drama

Get together with a few classmates to play charades. Use the words below or any of the vocabulary words you want to study. You can write the words on slips of paper and pick them out of a bowl or use your flash cards. One person picks a word, and the other people try to guess what word the person is acting out. You cannot use any words or sounds as you act out the word.

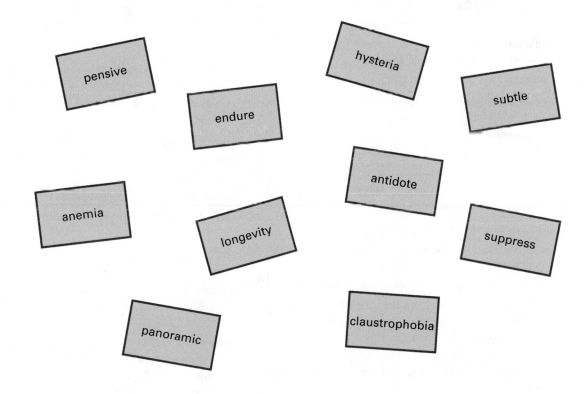

pensive · hysteria · subtle · endure · antidote · anemia · longevity · suppress · panoramic · claustrophobia

Glossary

abhor *v.* to detest; to loathe; to hate

acclaim *n.* enthusiastic approval or praise *v.* to applaud; to announce with enthusiastic approval

acronym *n.* a word or abbreviation formed from the initial letters or groups of letters of the words in a name or phrase

adage *n.* a traditional saying; a proverb

adhere *v.* 1. to follow closely   2. to give support 3. to stick together

adorn *v.* to decorate; to beautify

advocate *n.* a person who supports a cause *v.* to support or urge; to recommend

affinity *n.* fondness; attachment; liking

alibi *n.* an excuse or explanation, especially used to avoid blame

alliance *n.* an agreement to cooperate; an association

amiable *adj.* good-natured; agreeable

amnesia *n.* loss of memory, often from an illness or shock; forgetfulness

amorous *adj.* being in love; passionate

anemia *n.* a lack of oxygen-carrying material in the blood, which results in weakness

annihilate *v.* to destroy; to defeat completely

antidote *n.* 1. something that prevents an unwanted effect; a cure   2. a medicine or other remedy for counteracting the effects of a poison or a disease

antipathy *n.* an aversion; an opposition in feeling; dislike

apathy *n.* lack of interest; absence or suppression of emotion or excitement

assent *v.* to agree or concur   *n.* agreement, as to a proposal

asset *n.* a desirable thing or quality

avant-garde *adj.* experimental   *n.* the advanced group in a field

aversion *n.* 1. a strong dislike of something and a desire to avoid it; hatred   2. a cause or object of such a dislike

avert *v.* 1. to prevent   2. to turn away or aside

B

bane *n.* 1. something that ruins or spoils; irritation 2. death or destruction   3. a deadly poison

barbarian *n.* 1. a savage; a brute   2. a person without culture

berate *v.* to scold harshly; to criticize

bewilder *v.* to confuse, baffle, or puzzle

C

catharsis *n.* the relief of emotional tensions, especially through a work of art

charisma *n.* a special quality of leadership that inspires devotion; charm; allure

circumspection *n.* watchfulness; caution; care

circumvent *v.* 1. to go around   2. to avoid by cleverness; to elude

clandestine *adj.* secret; private

claustrophobia *n.* a fear of small or enclosed places

cliché *n.* a commonplace or overused expression or idea

colloquialism *n.* an expression used in conversational or informal language, not usually appropriate for formal writing

comprise *v.* 1. to consist of; to be composed of 2. to include; to contain; to form

concise *adj.* expressing much in a few words; brief

condone *v.* 1. to forgive or pardon; to excuse 2. to overlook; to ignore something illegal or offensive; to give unstated approval to

consensus *n.* unity of opinion; agreement; harmony

conservationist *n.* a person who works to save the environment; an environmentalist

convene   *v.* 1. to assemble, usually for a public purpose; to organize   2. to summon to appear

coup or **coup d'etat**   *n.* overthrow of the government; revolt

covert   *adj.* concealed; secret; disguised

credibility   *n.* trustworthiness; believability

credo   *n.* a formula of belief; a code or ritual

cupola   *n.* a dome or domelike structure

cursory   *adj.* going rapidly over something, without noticing details; hasty; superficial

D

decipher   *v.* to decode; to make out; to make sense of

decisive   *adj.* 1. definite; clear   2. displaying firmness; determined   3. crucial; important

deficiency   *n.* lack; shortage

definitive   *adj.* most reliable or complete

defraud   *v.* to take away a right, money, or property by deception; to cheat

delude   *v.* to mislead; to deceive; to fool

dependable   *adj.* trustworthy; responsible

depose   *v.* to remove from an important position or office; to dethrone

discreet   *adj.* careful; cautious

dissent   *v.* to differ in feeling or opinion, especially from the majority   *n.* a difference of opinion

domain   *n.* 1. an area of concern; a field   2. a territory of control; a realm

dour   *adj.* dismal; gloomy; forbidding

durable   *adj.* lasting; firm; permanent

E

eclectic   *adj.* selecting from various sources; diverse

edifice   *n.* a building or a structure, usually used when referring to a large or important building

ego   *n.* the conscious part of a person; self-esteem

elicit   *v.* to draw or bring out; to obtain

embellish   *v.* 1. to exaggerate; to elaborate; to add details   2. to decorate

emissary   *n.* 1. a representative sent on a mission; a delegate   2. an agent sent on a secret mission

encroachment   *n.* the act of gradually taking over an area or possessions that belong to someone else; an intrusion

endemic   *adj.* natural to a particular area; native

endow   *v.* 1. to furnish; to equip   2. to give money as a donation

endure   *v.* 1. to tolerate; to allow   2. to last

entrepreneur   *n.* one who assumes the risks of a business or enterprise

euphemism   *n.* the substitution of a mild or vague expression for one considered harsh

euphoria   *n.* a feeling of extreme well-being or extreme happiness

exemplify   *v.* to show by example; to model; to represent

F

façade   *n.* 1. exterior of a building, especially the front, and usually impressive   2. a false appearance

facilitate   *v.* to make easier; to assist

fertile   *adj.* 1. very productive   2. capable of having children

feudalism   *n.* a political system of the Middle Ages, based on holding land

figurehead   *n.* a person in a position of leadership who has no real power

finale   *n.* the concluding part of any performance; end

foresight   *n.* 1. concern for the future; carefulness   2. knowledge of the future

frenzied   *adj.* wild; agitated; mad

fresco   *n.* painting done on moist plaster

fruitful   *adj.* successful; abundant

G

gateway   *n.* 1. something that functions as an entrance or point of entry   2. a structure around an entrance that can be shut by a gate

glitch   *n.* a minor malfunction or technical error

H

habitat   *n.* 1. The environment where a plant or animal typically lives; surroundings   2. The place where something or someone is usually found

holistic   *adj.* 1. focusing on the importance of the whole and how its parts depend on each other   2. nontraditional health care

homage   *n.* honor; tribute

homonym   *n.* one of two or more words that have the same sound and sometimes the same spelling but differ in meaning

humanism   *n.* 1. philosophy emphasizing the importance of human interests and values, dating from the time of the Renaissance   2. study of the humanities (literature, languages, philosophy, art)

hysteria   *n.* emotional excess; nervous outburst; excitement

I

id *n.* the primitive, pleasure-loving, aggressive part of a person

impede *v.* to block; to hinder

impending *adj.* 1. about to happen; in the near future; approaching 2. threatening; looming

impose *v.* to force on others

incredulous *adj.* skeptical; doubtful; disbelieving

indicate *v.* 1. to be a sign of; to show the need for; to reveal 2. to point out or point to

infrastructure *n.* 1. foundations countries depend on, such as roads and power plants 2. the basic features of an organization

innate *adj.* 1. possessed at birth 2. possessed as an essential characteristic

intermittent *adj.* stopping and beginning again; periodic; irregular

intrigue *v.* to fascinate *n.* a scheme; a plot

irony *n.* 1. a clash between what is expected to happen and what really does, often used humorously in literature 2. the use of words to state the opposite of their precise meaning

J

jovial *adj.* merry; good-humored; cheerful

L

lax *adj.* not strict; careless; loose; vague

liability *n.* a disadvantage; an undesirable thing

longevity *n.* long life; length of life or service

M

mammal *n.* warm-blooded vertebrate (animal with a backbone)

medieval *adj.* of the Middle Ages

mercenary *adj.* selfish; greedy *n.* a professional soldier hired to fight in a foreign army

miscalculation *n.* a mistake in planning or forecasting

misgiving *n.* a feeling of doubt or distrust

modify *v.* to change the form of; to vary; to alter partially

moratorium *n.* suspension of an activity; an end or halt

N

naturopathic *adj.* treating diseases without drugs

niche *n.* 1. an appropriate place or position 2. a recess in a wall for a statue or other decorative object

nurture *v.* to educate or train *n.* the act of promoting development or growth; rearing

O

oblivious *adj.* unaware; forgetful

obsession *n.* an idea that excessively occupies the mind; a fascination

omnipotent *adj.* having great or unlimited authority or power

omnipresent *adj.* present everywhere at once

omnivorous *adj.* eating all types of foods

optimist *n.* a person who looks on the bright side; one who expects a positive result

ordeal *n.* a harsh or trying test or experience

ovation *n.* applause; approval

P

pandemonium *n.* disorder; chaos

panoramic *adj.* a wide view; scenic or pleasing

pensive *adj.* thoughtful; reflective

phishing *n.* the practice of luring innocent Internet users to a fake Web site by using real-looking e-mail with the intent to steal personal information or introduce a virus

plague *n.* 1. a widespread disease; an outbreak 2. any widespread evil; any annoyance *v.* to trouble; to annoy; to make miserable

plunder *v.* to rob by force, as in war; to raid

potential *n.* the ability for growth or development *adj.* possible but not yet realized

precise *adj.* 1. exact; accurate; definite 2. strictly correct; demanding

presentiment *n.* a feeling that something is about to happen, especially something bad; foreboding; expectation

privilege *n.* an advantage; a right

proclaim *v.* 1. to state publicly 2. to praise publicly 3. to prohibit publicly

proliferate *v.* to increase in number; spread rapidly; to grow

prominent *adj.* well known; leading; notable

propensity *n.* a tendency; a leaning; a preference

protocol *n.* 1. a code of correct behavior; the etiquette diplomats follow 2. a plan for a medical treatment or scientific experiment 3. computer science: a standard method for controlling data transmission between computers

provocative *adj.* stimulating; exciting; troubling

pseudonym   *n.* a fictitious name usually used by an author to conceal his or her identity; pen name

R

realm   *n.* 1. a territory ruled by a king or queen; an empire   2. an area of interest, knowledge, or activity

rectify   *v.* to correct; to put right; to fix

regime   *n.* government; period of time that a person or political system is in power

Renaissance   *n.* 1. a period of European history from the fourteenth to the seventeenth centuries in which there was renewed interest in learning and discovery   2. (small r) a rebirth; a revival

resourceful   *adj.* able to deal skillfully with new situations; capable; inventive

revitalize   *v.* to renew; to invigorate; to refresh

S

scrutinize   *v.* to examine carefully, especially looking for errors; to inspect

seclusion   *n.* solitude; a sheltered place

secular   *adj.* worldly; not holy or religious

serenity   *n.* peacefulness; tranquility

soliloquy   *n.* 1. a speech in a drama in which a character, alone or as if alone, expresses innermost thoughts   2. the act of talking while or as if alone

spam   *n.* junk e-mail; unasked for e-mail, often advertising, sent to multiple individuals   *v.* 1. to send unwanted e-mail   2. to send to multiple individuals   *n.* (capital S) a canned meat product made mainly from pork

subjugate   *v.* to conquer; to master; to dominate

subliminal   *adj.* understandable by the subconscious; hidden

submissive   *adj.* obedient; passive

subtle   *adj.* 1. not obvious; hard to see   2. difficult to understand; cunning; clever

superego   *n.* the moralistic part of a person

suppress   *v.* 1. to consciously inhibit an impulse or action; to repress   2. to abolish; to conquer   3. to withhold from publication; to censor

surpass   *v.* to go beyond; to excel; to be superior to

susceptible   *adj.* open to an influence; sensitive

syllabus   *n.* an outline or other brief statement on the content of a course

syndrome   *n.* a set of symptoms that belong to a disorder or disease

synopsis   *n.* a brief statement that gives a general idea; a summary

T

terminology   *n.* the study of terms for particular subjects; the terms belonging to a specialized subject; vocabulary

transcendent   *adj.* superior; going beyond ordinary limits

transitory   *adj.* not lasting; temporary

U

undermine   *v.* 1. to weaken or damage (such as health or morale) by small stages   2. to weaken or cause to collapse by removing basic supports; to dig or tunnel beneath

unparalleled   *adj.* unmatched; without equal

urban   *adj.* 1. concerned with a city   2. typical of a city or city life

V

validity   *n.* 1. authenticity; legal soundness   2. strength; authority

venture   *n.* a business enterprise; an undertaking involving risk   *v.* to brave; to take the risk of

virile   *adj.* masculine; manly; strong

virtual   *adj.* 1. created or run by a computer; simulated   2. almost existing; near; practical   3. existing in the mind

voyeurism   *n.* the act of watching others, especially secretively and usually related to sexual objects or acts

W

wrest   *v.* 1. to extract or take through force or continued effort   2. to misrepresent or twist the meaning or use of

Z

zealous   *adj.* enthusiastic; eager; passionate

zenith   *n.* the highest point; the peak; the top

zoology   *n.* the study of animals, including their behavior and development

Create Your Own Flash Cards

Using flash cards can be an immensely helpful way to study vocabulary words. The process of making the flash cards will aid you in remembering the meanings of the words. Index cards work well as flash cards, or you may use the following flash card templates to get you started. Put the word and the pronunciation on the front of the card. Elements you may want to include on the back of the card will vary according to the word and your preferred learning style. Consider the ideas below and find what works best for you.

1. **The part of speech:** Write an abbreviation for the part of speech, such as *n.* for noun or *v.* for verb. This addition will help when you are writing sentences.
2. **A simple definition:** Use the definitions in the book or modify them to something that has meaning for you. Use a definition you can remember.
3. **A sentence:** Make up your own sentence that correctly uses the word. Try to use a context clue to help you remember the word. It might help to put yourself or friends in the sentences to personalize your use of the word. If you really like a sentence from the book, you can use that too.
4. **A drawing:** If you are a visual learner, try drawing the word. Some words especially lend themselves to this method. Your drawing doesn't have to be fancy; it should just help you remember the meaning of the word.
5. **A mnemonic [ni mon′ ik] device:** These are methods to help your memory. They can be rhymes, formulas, or clues. For example: Stationery with an *e* is the kind that goes in an *e*nvelope. Make up any connections you can between the word and its meaning.
6. **Highlight word parts:** Circle one or more word parts (prefixes, roots, or suffixes) that appear in the word and write the meaning(s) next to the word part: for example, (fin)ale. See the Word Parts chapters in the text for more on word parts.

→ end

Whatever you do, make the cards personally meaningful. Find the techniques that work for you, and use them in creating your cards. Then make the time to study the cards. Carry them with you, and study them any chance you get. Also, find someone who will be tough in quizzing you with the cards. Have the person hold up a card, and you give the meaning and use the word in a sentence. Don't quit until you are confident that you know what each word means.

Sample card

Front

Back

surpass

[sər pas′]

v. to go beyond; to excel   (I did it!)

I surpassed my expectations when I climbed the mountain.